The
politicization of
the Supreme Court

MAY 08 2024

At Issue

The Politicization of
the Supreme Court

Other Books in the At Issue Series

At Issue

The Politicization of
the Supreme Court

Eamon Doyle, Book Editor

GREENHAVEN
PUBLISHING

Published in 2022 by Greenhaven Publishing, LLC
353 3rd Avenue, Suite 255, New York, NY 10010

Articles in Greenhaven Publishing anthologies are often edited for length to meet page
requirements. In addition, original titles of these works are changed to clearly present
the main thesis and to explicitly indicate the author's opinion. Every effort is made to
ensure that Greenhaven Publishing accurately reflects the original intent of the authors.
Every effort has been made to trace the owners of the copyrighted material.

Cover image: Joe Ravi/Shutterstock.com

Library of Congress Cataloging-in-Publication Data
Names: Doyle, Eamon, 1988- editor.
Title: The politicization of the Supreme Court / Eamon Doyle, book editor.
Description: First edition. | New York, NY : Greenhaven Publishing, LLC,
     [2022] | Series: At issue | Includes bibliographical references and
     index. |
     Audience: Ages 15+ | Audience: Grades 10–12 | Summary: "Anthology of
     diverse viewpoints exploring the Supreme Court's politicization across
     history, whether it is realistic or useful to expect it to be insulated
     from politics, and possible means of depoliticizing the court"—
     Provided by publisher.
Identifiers: LCCN 2020055630 | ISBN 9781534508200 (library binding) | ISBN
     9781534508194 (paperback) | ISBN 9781534508217 (ebook)
Subjects: LCSH: United States. Supreme Court—Political activity—Juvenile
     literature. | Political questions and judicial power—United
     States—Juvenile literature.
Classification: LCC KF8742 . P65 2022 | DDC 347.73/26—dc23
LC record available at https://lccn.loc.gov/2020055630

Manufactured in the United States of America

Website: http://greenhavenpublishing.com

Contents

Introduction

The United States Constitution sets forth a government divided into three branches—legislative, executive, and judicial— and a system of checks and balances intended to facilitate an equilibrium of power between the three branches. The Supreme Court, established by Article III of the Constitution, stands at the head of the judicial branch and represents the final authority in the US legal system. The court has jurisdiction over appellate proceedings in both state and federal court and the authority to conduct judicial review of statutes and presidential directives. The latter authorities provide the means for the court to check and restrain actions by the legislative and executive branches.

In theory, the judicial branch is the least political of the three branches. Federal judges are appointed rather than elected to ensure that their decisions are shielded from political considerations. But their actions are not intended to be arbitrary or subjective; rather, the expectation is that judges and judicial officials will utilize legal/constitutional reasoning and practice an ethic that legal professionals refer to as "judicial independence." US lawyer Steven H. Aden elaborates in the following:

> *Judicial independence is the crowning glory of the American constitutional system, and the Supreme Court's singular commitment to the Constitution and laws of the Republic—with its concomitant determination to avoid political entanglements—is the brightest jewel in that crown. […] Federal courts have no army at their command, no police force to enforce their decrees. The Rule of Law doesn't just depend upon respect for the courts—it is respect for the courts. Federal judges—alone among federal officials—have lifetime tenure in their jobs to insulate themselves from pressures that would inevitably arise from the need to stand for election or to secure political appointment or re-appointment. For this reason, the Supreme Court ought to be respected in its inurement from the political forces that—by constitutional design—perpetually*

crash like storm waves against the Congress and the president. Once the Justices begin to decide disputes with an eye toward the impact their decisions may have on the country's often-heated political discourse, not only the trust reposed on the judicial system by litigants, but even more importantly the meaning of the law itself—of federal statutes and constitutional provisions—is subject to distortion for political ends.[1]

Aden's description illustrates how foundational the expectation of judicial independence is to the American system of government—and what types of risk are likely to emerge if the expectation loses strength.

In addition to the expectation of judicial independence, democratic theory calls for some self-restraint on the part of the judiciary—thus allowing the will of the people to express itself in the legislative and executive branches with minimal interference. Legal theorists often refer to this ethic as "judicial modesty":

Officially, US Supreme Court justices (and especially nominees to the court during their confirmation hearings) subscribe to a doctrine of "judicial modesty," which suggests that—in a democracy—the least democratic branch should overrule the policy preferences of the more democratic branches only when the conflict between a law and the Constitution is strong and clear and never when the justices simply have a different policy preference from the legislators. Trouble is, no one can define or enforce those limits other than the justices themselves. When they impose their policy preferences in the guise of defending the Constitution—or even when they are perceived to be doing so—the credibility of the whole system takes a hit.[2]

Some historians have argued that the court is not and was never quite as apolitical as the theory suggests, pointing both to deep connections between constitutional jurisprudence and political theory and to acrimonious confirmation proceedings throughout US history.

However, most observers agree that over the past three decades, the court has become increasingly politicized and increasingly subject to messy partisan dynamics in the legislature. The following quote from liberal activist Miles Mogulescu exemplifies a perspective that is common among supporters of the Democratic Party:

> *[Republican Senate Majority Leader Mitch] McConnell has already broken the norms beyond recognition. In concert with the right-wing Federalist Society and Heritage Foundation, McConnell has devoted the past 30 years to packing the Federal Courts with increasingly reactionary ideologues. Among the right-wing decisions decided by a bare 5-4 conservative majority are the 2000 decision to stop the Florida recount and install George W. Bush as President, the decision to gut key sections of the Voting Rights Act, the refusal to put limits on partisan gerrymandering, and* Citizens United. *By a single vote majority, the Supreme Court has spent the past several decades undermining American democracy.*[3]

Republicans, on the other hand, tend to focus on the 1973 *Roe v. Wade* decision—which they view as an example of unconstitutional judicial overreach—and Democratic resistance to President George W. Bush's judicial appointments. As is often the case in political arguments like this, there is blame on both sides:

> *Many Democrats regard court-packing as justified retaliation for the GOP's "theft" of the Supreme Court seat that went to Neil Gorsuch as a result of the Republican-controlled Senate's refusal to hold hearings and vote on Barack Obama nominee Merrick Garland. Republicans, in turn, argue that their treatment of Garland was justified by past Democratic misdeeds in the judicial nomination process (including refusal to hold hearings for a number of prominent GOP circuit court nominees), and that the Democrats themselves had signaled they would refuse to consider a GOP nominee in circumstances similar to those surrounding the Garland appointment. The truth is that, for a long time, both parties have shamelessly violated a variety of norms surrounding judicial nominations almost any time it seemed like they might gain an advantage to doing so. And both are equally*

shameless in shifting back and forth on procedural issues whenever the political winds dictate.[4]

American politics stands at a major historical crossroads. Political polarization and partisan animosity are on the rise; the country faces a growing number of complex and urgent challenges; both of the major political parties are undergoing rapid transformations. The diverse and provocative viewpoints in *At Issue: The Politicization of the Supreme Court* address these issues as they relate to the Supreme Court of the United States. The institutional integrity of the Supreme Court is as important today as it has ever been in American history, and it is likely to be at the center of whatever historical developments we see over the next several years.

Endnotes

1. "Politics and the Supreme Court," by Steven H. Aden, *National Review*, September 17, 2019.
2. "How the Supreme Court Has Come to Play a Policymaking Role," by Eric Black, *MinnPost*, November 20, 2012.
3. "Expanding Supreme Court May Be Only Way to Protect Democracy," by Miles Mogulescu, OurFuture, March 14, 2019.
4. "The Case Against Court-Packing Revisited," by Ilya Somin, Reason Foundation, July 3, 2018.

1

The United States Has Become More Politically Polarized

Pew Research Center

The Pew Research Center is a nonpartisan think tank and one of the top sources for public opinion polling data in the United States.

This viewpoint examines the increasing degree of political polarization in contemporary American society and its effect on governance at the federal level. Partisan polarization and enmity have been on the rise in the United States since the early 1990s, but there are competing theories about what factors are driving the trend. The viewpoint looks deeper into the demography and behavior of partisan actors to uncover the hidden background—ideological, economic, engagement-based—of political polarization in America.

Republicans and Democrats are more divided along ideological lines—and partisan antipathy is deeper and more extensive—than at any point in the last two decades. These trends manifest themselves in myriad ways, both in politics and in everyday life. And a new survey of 10,000 adults nationwide finds that these divisions are greatest among those who are the most engaged and active in the political process.

The overall share of Americans who express consistently conservative or consistently liberal opinions has doubled over the past two decades from 10% to 21%. And ideological thinking

"Political Polarization in the American Public," Pew Research Center, June 12, 2014. Reprinted by permission.

is now much more closely aligned with partisanship than in the past. As a result, ideological overlap between the two parties has diminished: Today, 92% of Republicans are to the right of the median Democrat, and 94% of Democrats are to the left of the median Republican.

Partisan animosity has increased substantially over the same period. In each party, the share with a highly negative view of the opposing party has more than doubled since 1994. Most of these intense partisans believe the opposing party's policies "are so misguided that they threaten the nation's well-being."

"Ideological silos" are now common on both the left and right. People with down-the-line ideological positions—especially conservatives—are more likely than others to say that most of their close friends share their political views. Liberals and conservatives disagree over where they want to live, the kind of people they want to live around and even whom they would welcome into their families.

And at a time of increasing gridlock on Capitol Hill, many on both the left and the right think the outcome of political negotiations between Obama and Republican leaders should be that their side gets more of what it wants.

These sentiments are not shared by all—or even most—Americans. The majority do not have uniformly conservative or liberal views. Most do not see either party as a threat to the nation. And more believe their representatives in government should meet halfway to resolve contentious disputes rather than hold out for more of what they want.

Yet many of those in the center remain on the edges of the political playing field, relatively distant and disengaged, while the most ideologically oriented and politically rancorous Americans make their voices heard through greater participation in every stage of the political process.

The rise of ideological uniformity has been much more pronounced among those who are the most politically active. Today, almost four-in-ten (38%) politically engaged Democrats are consistent liberals, up from just 8% in 1994. The change among Republicans since then appears less dramatic—33% express consistently conservative views, up from 23% in the midst of the 1994 "Republican Revolution." But a decade ago, just 10% of politically engaged Republicans had across-the-board conservative attitudes.

On measure after measure—whether primary voting, writing letters to officials, volunteering for or donating to a campaign—the most politically polarized are more actively involved in politics, amplifying the voices that are the least willing to see the parties meet each other halfway.

These are among the findings of the largest study of US political attitudes ever undertaken by the Pew Research Center. Data are drawn from a national telephone survey of 10,013 adults, conducted from January through March of this year, and an ongoing series of follow-up surveys. This rich dataset, coupled with trends and insights from two decades of Pew Research Center polling, reveals a complex picture of partisan polarization and how it manifests itself in political behaviors, policy debates, election dynamics and everyday life.

What Polarization Looks Like

To chart the progression of ideological thinking, responses to 10 political values questions asked on multiple Pew Research surveys since 1994 have been combined to create a measure of ideological consistency. Over the past twenty years, the number of Americans in the "tails" of this ideological distribution has doubled from 10% to 21%. Meanwhile, the center has shrunk: 39% currently take a roughly equal number of liberal and conservative positions. That is down from about half (49%) of the public in surveys conducted in 1994 and 2004.

And this shift represents both Democrats moving to the left and Republicans moving to the right, with less and less overlap between the parties. Today, 92% of Republicans are to the right of the median (middle) Democrat, compared with 64% twenty years ago. And 94% of Democrats are to the left of the median Republican, up from 70% in 1994.

More Negative Views of the Opposing Party

Beyond the rise in ideological consistency, another major element in polarization has been the growing contempt that many Republicans and Democrats have for the opposing party. To be sure, disliking the other party is nothing new in politics. But today, these sentiments are broader and deeper than in the recent past.

In 1994, hardly a time of amicable partisan relations, a majority of Republicans had unfavorable impressions of the Democratic Party, but just 17% had very unfavorable opinions. Similarly, while most Democrats viewed the GOP unfavorably, just 16% had very unfavorable views. Since then, highly negative views have more than doubled: 43% of Republicans and 38% of Democrats now view the opposite party in strongly negative terms.

Even these numbers tell only part of the story. Those who have a very unfavorable impression of each party were asked: "Would you say the party's policies are so misguided that they threaten the nation's well-being, or wouldn't you go that far?" Most who were asked the question said yes, they would go that far. Among all Democrats, 27% say the GOP is a threat to the well-being of the country. That figure is even higher among Republicans, 36% of whom think Democratic policies threaten the nation.

Politics Gets Personal

Liberals and conservatives share a passion for politics. They are far more likely than those with more mixed ideological views to discuss politics on a weekly or daily basis. But for many, particularly on the right, those conversations may not include much in the way of opposing opinions.

Nearly two-thirds (63%) of consistent conservatives and about half (49%) of consistent liberals say most of their close friends share their political views. Among those with mixed ideological values, just 25% say the same. People on the right and left also are more likely to say it is important to them to live in a place where most people share their political views, though again, that desire is more widespread on the right (50%) than on the left (35%).

And while few Americans overall go so far as to voice disappointment with the prospect of a family member marrying a Democrat (8%) or a Republican (9%), that sentiment is not uncommon on the left or the right. Three-out-of-ten (30%) consistent conservatives say they would be unhappy if an immediate family member married a Democrat and about a quarter (23%) of across-the-board liberals say the same about the prospect of a Republican in-law.

To be sure, there are areas of consensus. Most Americans, regardless of their ideological preferences, value communities in which they would live close to extended family and high-quality schools. But far more liberals than conservatives think it is important that a community have racial and ethnic diversity (76% vs. 20%). At the same time, conservatives are more likely than liberals to attach importance to living in a place where many people share their religious faith (57% vs. 17% of liberals).

And the differences between right and left go beyond disagreements over politics, friends and neighbors. If they could choose anywhere to live, three-quarters of consistent conservatives prefer a community where "the houses are larger and farther apart, but schools, stores, and restaurants are several miles away." The preferences of consistent liberals are almost the exact inverse, with 77% saying they'd chose to live where "the houses are smaller and closer to each other, but schools, stores, and restaurants are within walking distance."

Polarization's Consequences

When they look at a political system in which little seems to get done, most Americans in the center of the electorate think that Obama and Republican leaders should simply meet each other halfway in addressing the issues facing the nation.

Yet an equitable deal is in the eye of the beholder, as both liberals and conservatives define the optimal political outcome as one in which their side gets more of what it wants. A majority of consistent conservatives (57%) say the ideal agreement between President Obama and congressional Republicans is one in which GOP leaders hold out for more of their goals. Consistent liberals take the opposite view: Their preferred terms (favored by 62%) end up closer to Obama's position than the GOP's.

Polarization in Red and Blue

The signs of political polarization are evident on both ends of the political spectrum, though the trajectory, nature and extent differ from left to right.

With Barack Obama in the White House, partisan antipathy is more pronounced among Republicans, especially consistently conservative Republicans. Overall, more Republicans than Democrats see the opposing party's policies as a threat and the differences are even greater when ideology is taken into account. Fully 66% of consistently conservative Republicans think the Democrats' policies threaten the nation's well-being. By comparison, half (50%) of consistently liberal Democrats say Republican policies jeopardize the nation's well-being. Conservatives also exhibit more partisan behavior in their personal lives; they are the most likely to have friends and prefer communities of like-minded people.

However, there is as much ideological uniformity on the left as the right. The share of Democrats holding consistently liberal views has grown steadily over the past 20 years, quadrupling from 5% in 1994 to 23% today. Social issues like homosexuality and immigration that once drove deep divides within the Democratic Party are now areas of relative consensus. And Democrats have become more uniformly critical of business and more supportive of government.

Changes in ideological consistency on the right have followed a different course. In 1994, during the "Republican Revolution," 13% of Republicans were consistent conservatives. That figure fell to 6% a decade later during George W. Bush's presidency, before rebounding to 20% today. This increase has come despite more moderate views among Republicans on issues like homosexuality and immigration, as GOP thinking on issues related to government and the economy has veered sharply to the right.

About the Study

This is the first report of a multi-part series based on a national survey of 10,013 adults nationwide, conducted January 23–March 16, 2014 by the Pew Research Center. The survey, funded in part through grants from the William and Flora Hewlett Foundation, the John D. and Catherine T. MacArthur Foundation and supported by the generosity of Don C. and Jeane M. Bertsch, is aimed at understanding the nature and scope of political polarization in the American public, and how it interrelates with government, society and people's personal lives.

The second report, coming in a few weeks, is the new Pew Research Center Political Typology. The typology—the sixth such study since 1987—looks beyond Red vs. Blue divisions to gain a clearer understanding of the dynamic nature of the "center" of the American electorate, and the internal divides on both the left and the right.

Later, the project will explore the various factors that contribute to political polarization, or stem from it. A September report will examine how political polarization is linked to people's information environments: Their news sources, social media habits and interpersonal communication networks. Other reports will look at how political polarization relates to where people live, to their political environments, to how they view themselves and others around them, to their socioeconomic circumstances, to generational changes and to broader sociological and psychological personality traits.

The current report is divided into five parts: The first two focus on measuring the nature and scope of political polarization, emphasizing the difference between growing ideological consistency and rising partisan antipathy. The third looks closely at how polarization manifests itself in people's personal lives.

The fourth looks at the relationship between polarization and practical policymaking, and the fifth digs deeper into how political participation both amplifies and reflects polarization.

About the Data

The data in this report are based on two independent survey administrations with the same randomly selected, nationally representative group of respondents. The first is the center's largest survey on domestic politics to date: the 2014 Political Polarization and Typology Survey, a national telephone survey of 10,013 adults, on landlines and cell phones, from January through March of this year. The second involved impaneling a subset of these respondents into the newly created American Trends Panel and following up with them via a survey conducted by web and telephone.

2

The Supreme Court Shapes (and Is Shaped by) Its Public Support

Matt Grossmann

Matt Grossmann is director of the Institute for Public Policy and Social Research and associate professor of political science at Michigan State University.

This viewpoint is an excerpted transcript of a podcast conducted by Matt Grossmann and featuring political scientists Alison Higgins Merrill and Michael Nelson. Merrill finds that support for the Supreme Court is high but declining, partially in response to ideological trends. Nelson finds that public support for the Supreme Court is relatively stable and that most people's negative reactions to decisions don't last. Both featured guests discuss what we can learn from Chief Justice John Roberts and the court after the conclusion of the latest term.

Matt Grossmann: The Supreme Court finished its term with a flood of momentous decisions, tacking surprisingly leftward, with Chief Justice John Roberts crafting most of the majorities and the court agreeing with public opinion nearly all of the time. Is the court worried about its public nonpartisan stature and does it need to be?

Today, I talked to Alison Higgins Merrill, Susquehanna University, about her ongoing research, including a paper with Kathryn Haglin, Soren Jordan and Joseph Daniel Ura, "Ideology and Public Support for the Supreme Court." She finds that support for the Supreme Court is declining partially in response to ideological trends. I also talked to Michael Nelson at Penn State University about his research, including a new *Journal of Politics* paper with Patrick Tucker, "The Stability of the US Supreme Court's Legitimacy." He finds that public support for the Supreme Court is relatively stable and most people's reactions don't last. Nelson says that the Supreme Court independence is popular and hard to budge.

Michael Nelson: We have done a bunch of surveys that ask Americans the same set of questions about their willingness to tolerate some fundamental changes to the US Supreme Court. That's everything from totally abolishing the court, to getting rid of the court's ability to decide particular types of cases or to make the court less independent.

Some of the strongest evidence we have is from a panel survey of Americans during the Obama administration. So, during the last four years of the Obama administration, the same people answered these questions a couple or more times a year, and then we can look within person over time. And what we find is, especially at the aggregate level, the responses on those questions have stayed the same over time. Most people are not willing to, or say they're not willing to, tolerate the court being meddled with. And that didn't really change that much, even as the court decided things like same sex marriage during the second half of the Obama presidency.

Matt Grossmann: The court usually sides with the public and might not have much capacity to influence it.

Michael Nelson: If we go way back to what we learned in elementary school we think about the court as being a unique type of political institution because it's countermajoritary. In other words, that the court can stand in opposition to public opinion when it needs to. And in reality, that's not really the case. Most of the evidence suggests that the court's decisions, particularly on important issues, tend to be congruent with public opinion. So for example, the case that the court decided a week or so ago about sex discrimination and whether you can discriminate against gay and lesbian employees. They held that you couldn't, and that's actually a decision that's congruent with what most Americans want.

So there's this idea that the court will stand in opposition to public opinion, but in reality, the court's decisions tend to be pretty congruent with public opinion.

There's also another literature about the extent to which the court can change people's opinions. So in other words, I have an idea about a policy issue, the court rules, and does my opinion change? And that literature comes to a lot more mixed conclusions, in part because people really vary in the extent to which they pay attention to the court and the court, particularly this time of year, usually the end of June, beginning of July, when it decides its most important cases, they tend to kind of go both ways. So we've seen some big wins for liberals like in the sex discrimination case and in the abortion case this year, but also some cases that have come out in a strong, conservative direction regarding regulation and things like that.

So there's pretty strong evidence that the court's decisions tend to be in line with public opinion, weaker evidence about the court's ability to change people's opinions,

Matt Grossmann: But Merrill says people's support for the court declines when it moves in the other ideological direction, particularly for conservatives.

Alison Higgins Merrill: The most recent projects that I've been working on with Kathryn Haglin, Soren Jordan and Joe Ura, are looking at asymmetries in public evaluations of the Supreme Court.

And what kind of got us started on this project was that we were noticing that when you look at approval for the Supreme Court, there were differences in what conservatives were saying, versus what liberals were saying. And so we wanted to unpack that a little bit more. What we actually found, which was really cool, is that as the Supreme Court decision-making diverges from the public's immediately preferred level, policy liberalism, so how much involvement the government has in citizens day-to-day lives, how much that the public is willing to tolerate the government helping you out, the support for the court declines, but in different ways for conservatives than for liberals.

And this actually really got started because of a recent Lupton, Smallpage, and Enders article, which shows that American political values really do operate asymmetrically among ideological groups, and those ideological groups, the conservatives, the liberals really do map onto our two major political parties, the Republicans and the Democrats, and specifically, when we look at conservatives, we tend to see that these values are more concentrated and they tend to be emphasizing things like individualism, personal liberty and moral absolutism, versus liberalism, which is a much more diverse coalition of beliefs. And it's really coalesced among a more diverse coalition of social groups as well, that tend to support more egalitarianism and more relativism.

And so what we noticed was that when we kind of broke it down that way, conservatives tend to experience much more intense response to political stimuli than liberals. And this is something that we've seen in the literature in other areas of American politics before. So for example, changes in domestic spending tends to affect Democrats less than it affects Republicans. And what we did is we kind of took these different pieces and created this theoretical argument that in the aggregate, so if we're looking more big picture, specific support for the Supreme court is more strongly related to the perception that the court is overly liberal, than the perception that the court is overly conservative. In other words, when the court is perceived as being too liberal, support wanes a lot more quickly among conservatives. So conservatives are more likely to jump ship and express disapproval of the Supreme Court, when they think the court has moved in a more liberal direction than liberals.

And what we found when we started taking apart this data was that we were actually correct. The decline in public support for the court in recent years is more heavily related to the result of changing attitudes among conservatives than among liberals. And we kind of also noticed that when we have a democratic president, 33% of Americans judge the court to be too liberal, versus when we have a Republican president, only about 25% of the public judges the court is being too liberal.

So it's also connected to evaluations of the president as well as who is in office and evaluations of Congress as well. However, if the public approves of Congress, they're also more likely to approve of the Supreme Court.

It's just kind of interesting that we're seeing these differences in evaluations among different groups of Americans. And so generally the court enjoys more support than the other two branches of government, and I think a lot of this is just, there's this mystique around the Supreme Court, people don't understand it the way that they might understand Congress and the presidency, and this might be because they were unelected. But we're still seeing differences in evaluations of the court among conservatives and liberals.

Matt Grossmann: Supreme Court support is high but dropping.

Alison Higgins Merrill: Compared to the other branches of government, the court tends to enjoy support at levels over 50%. So more than half of the public at any given point tends to approve of the job the court is doing. And this is typically measured by the Gallup question: Do you approve or disapprove of the way the Supreme Court is handling their job? And you can interchange the president or Congress for the Supreme Court in that question.

So we use that to kind of measure support amongst the three branches of government.

However, in the past, I think it's five years, we've seen support for the court dip below that 50% threshold, which is a little troubling to not only members of the federal judiciary, but people who study the court. It's like, "All right, why all of a sudden are we seeing this decrease in support for the court?"

And if you compare it to the president, President Trump has struggled to get over 40% approval for the majority of his presidency. He's been sitting right at that 38 to 41 percentage approval for most of his first term in office, and Congress is even lower. I think one of the lows recently has been 11% approval for Congress. It's gone up a little bit and they're in the high teens to low 20s. So comparatively, the court's looking great compared to the other two branches of government.

Matt Grossmann: Nelson says, the individual and aggregate trends might not match if the court's moves are balanced.

Michael Nelson: The big thing to emphasize is, just because something is stable in the aggregate, doesn't mean that nothing's happening on the individual level. So even in those panel data that I was talking about earlier where we surveyed the same people over time, a lot of individual people would bounce around a bit and that bouncing around, really the only thing that predicted it was their ideology. But at the same time, because the court we've observed over the past couple decades has been a court whose major decisions throw some positive decisions to the liberals and some positive for conservatives, those things kind of balance out in the aggregate. To the extent people are paying attention, if I'm a conservative, I see a couple of conservative decisions, I like that; I see a couple liberal decisions, I don't like those, and it goes in the other way. And so in the aggregate those things can balance out, even if there's individual level change.

Matt Grossmann: And Merrill agrees that the micro level is important to combine with the macro level.

Alison Higgins Merrill: I think Michael's research at the individual level is super informative for how we understand those micro level components and why we see stability and enduring support for our institutions in general. But I also think that taking my research and the research I've been working on with my co-authors at the aggregate level and pairing it with some of the more micro level approaches gives us a better sense of why we see short term fluctuations, but long term support.

And so in the short run route, we might see pushback against the Supreme Court, but it's going to moderate itself and it's going to revert back to those existing high levels of support because the court is an institution, people like it, they respect it, they think highly of it. It might be that they're pissed off about a particular issue, but at the end of the day, they still really like the institution as it is. So it's all right. Well, that made me upset and I don't necessarily like the way it happened, and so I'm going to maybe take my frustration out and say that I disapprove of the job they're doing and maybe vote for politicians that are deciding things in line with my preferences that might influence the justices in some negative way, but eventually I might just agree with the Supreme Court in general.

And we've seen this in the literature. There was a very negative and harsh criticism of both *Brown v. Board of Education* and *Roe v. Wade*, but over time, the majority of the public has come to support those decisions. And so it's kind of like the court is leading public opinion. They're like, "We know you might disagree with us now and be really unhappy, but eventually you're going to like the fact that we put these safeguards in place."

And so I think taking the macro level research that people like Michael have done with some of the more aggregate level stuff, kind of helps us understand that push and pull that comes with short term versus long term support.

Matt Grossmann: Nelson says, "Much of the public is not paying that much attention and doesn't necessarily see the big ideological trends."

Michael Nelson: The issue here is the extent to which people are really tuned into what the court is doing. For a certain set of people who are pretty politically sophisticated, they can look and know that during the Trump presidency, Anthony Kennedy, who was the justice, who was the median justice, stepped down, he was replaced by somebody who's much more conservative, it seems. And now we have Chief Justice Roberts in the middle of the court, which moved the median member of the court to the right.

The thing that's tricky for that to have an effect on public opinion is that the public has to realize that that all happened. That's pretty complicated for most people, particularly because the most important cases of the year tend to come out some for liberals and some for conservatives. And so one interesting thing from a research perspective over the next few years is that it looks like the court's policymaking will on-balance move to be more one-sided than it had been in the past few decades, and so we'll be able to observe the change that more single-sided type of policymaking has on people's support for the court.

Matt Grossmann: And it's not clear who the court needs to be following; the public or the elites.

Michael Nelson: I also studied state Supreme Courts, where most of the justices have to stand for reelection. And there, there's kind of an obvious reason why you would expect courts to follow public opinion, which is that for most state Supreme Court justices, if you make a bunch of decisions that a majority of people don't like, then a majority of people are going to support somebody else in the next election. Supreme Court justices on the other hand, don't have any real institutional reason to need to follow public opinion, at least at the mass level, and so we might think that they're more attuned to, say, congressional preferences or something because Congress can control their budget and things like that.

The thing that makes it hard to disentangle responsiveness to different audiences, especially for the Supreme Court, is that a lot of the policies that tend to be popular among the American people are also popular among elected officials. And surprisingly, there's pretty little evidence that the general ideological tenor of the court's decisions changes as the court gets closer or further in ideological distance from Congress.

Matt Grossmann: We don't know if the court really needs that public support and whether bad opinions would kill them.

Michael Nelson: The story goes that the Supreme Court more than any other political institution really needs this public support, that if the court's decisions veer off in one direction or something else happens that causes the court to lose its legitimacy, then for example, its decisions could not be implemented and there'd be no electoral repercussions. But the problem with testing that is that we've pretty much only observed a court that has been broadly supported by the American people and the court hasn't really taken any wild and crazy actions that has caused us to see kind of spikes downward in its popularity or its support.

And so it's kind of hard to say because the court itself is strategic. We have lots of theory that suggests it would be really bad for the court. The court has written in some of its opinions that it would be bad for them if they lost public support. At least some justices say they believe that. But we don't really have that much variation on the public support for the court to really know much about it.

[...]

Matt Grossmann: Merrill points out that the Supreme Court has big choices about how to address each issue by taking specific cases.

Alison Higgins Merrill: The justices, I think they pay attention more to the issues than they might to particular cases. And I can't remember the exact quotation, but I remember reading something that justice Sotomayor had said about justice Scalia when he was giving her advice on certiorari petitions during her first term. And he said, "Hey, if we miss it in one case, we'll get it in another case because we get thousands of questions that deal with the same issue." And so I think they're a little bit more concerned about dealing with issues than maybe specific cases. Whereas I think the American public wants them to do the specific case and maybe not the issue.

[…]

Matt Grossmann: It is a threat to the court if they appear political, and Trump isn't helping that. But Nelson says the public might not be very influenced by Trump's tweets complaining about it.

Michael Nelson: There's a good bit of evidence out there that suggests that one of the biggest threats to the court's legitimacy, perhaps even bigger than whether people like the decisions or not is whether or not they think the court's being political in its decisions. And what we mean by that is not that Ruth Bader Ginsburg votes liberally, Brett Kavanaugh votes conservatively. Most people get that they have views on important policy issues as everyday Americans.

It's not strange that Supreme Court justices are also going to have opinions on those issues. We don't see people punish the court that much, if they think the justices vote on policy grounds. Where we see them punish the court is when they think the justices are engaging in self-dealing or they're bargaining or being strategic, all the stuff that people don't like about Congress. And so the worry about Trump, when Trump was tweeting about the court was whether or not Trump's tweets were going to contaminate the court in the sense that he was drawing them into this politicized arena. And it doesn't really seem like he does. It seems like he tweets about so much stuff all the time, and he's disliked by so many people that if I'm somebody who doesn't like Trump. And I see his tweet. It might even make me like the court more because I'm programmed to like things that Trump doesn't like. On the other hand, if I'm somebody who does support Trump, he can't hurt my support for the court. But again, because Trump's approval at baseline is so low, he hasn't been able to really harm the court support that much with his tweets.

[…]

Matt Grossmann: So what's next? Merrill says litigants will respond to recent ideological trends on the court.

Alison Higgins Merrill: To a lot of lower court judges, I don't think this is particularly surprising. I think that, again, it's Roberts deciding in line with his role as the chief justice and managing the court as this institution. But for litigants, I think this is going to affect the types of cases that are being brought before the court, because a lot of the abortion challenges now … Two times in the past four years has the court struck down really excessive state laws that they have said unduly burden a woman who wants to receive an abortion in her home state. And so I think that's going to put the kibosh a little bit on states either passing really restrictive laws or litigants pursuing resolution at the highest court, because they've seen now twice that the court has struck down those state laws. And so that might slow some of the abortion challenges that we see.

And I think the slap on the wrist that the court has given the Trump administration recently might also impact which cases the federal government decides to bring to the Supreme Court and how those are addressed at the lower levels as well. Because this court is not going to be exactly what the administration had hoped it would be. And so it's going to cause them to rethink their strategy and how they go about drafting executive orders and other legislation that the court would potentially rule on. So I think we might see a little slow down in some of those areas as well.

Matt Grossmann: And Nelson says we keep thinking the balanced court will change, and perhaps it finally will, after the next election,

Michael Nelson: It was boring for a long time, because the court seemed like it was pretty four-four with somebody in the middle who is pretty wobbly. And I remember literally the day that Justice Scalia passed away and Obama was in office, it was like, "Oh wow. We're finally going to get to observe what happens when you have a strong liberal majority in contemporary America." And then that didn't happen. And then we were all talking about how now, with Roberts, we don't really have a swing justice anymore. He's median, but he won't swing to the liberals in these important cases. And then he did that. So we keep thinking that maybe we're going to get to observe something that is new and different, but that hasn't happened so far. And I guess we'll know a lot more in four years, whether that was just a fluke of the times or whether that's just the way that the court operates.

3

Increasing Politicization of the Supreme Court Is a Danger to the Nation's Democratic Principles

Center for American Progress

The Center for American Progress is an independent, nonpartisan public policy research and advocacy organization based in Washington, DC. The organization is dedicated to promoting and advancing progressive values in American life.

This viewpoint from 2007 provides a window into an earlier era in American politics, when the Supreme Court was less politicized. Even though the authors are concerned about the partisan mindset of then president George W. Bush's two nominees, they quote Democrats who were willing to vote for their confirmation as trusting in the process ("Today I will vote my hopes and not my fears"). Such accommodation reflected what was once a fairly bipartisan commitment to judicial impartiality and rule-of-law principles. As the authors of this article detail, the strength of our collective commitment to those principles may be fading.

A t the outset of the still-unfolding scandal over the firing of nine United States attorneys and the politicization of the hiring process at the Department of Justice, Attorney General Alberto Gonzales was adamant that he would "never, ever" replace a United States attorney for political reasons. Deputy Attorney

"The Politicization of the Supreme Court," Center for American Progress, June 28, 2007. Reprinted by permission.

General Paul McNulty called the allegation of politicization at the DOJ "like a knife to my heart." Now we know that political officials at DOJ "crossed the line" many times in an effort to place "loyal Bushies" in positions of power.

Unfortunately, a similar story appears to be unfolding at the Supreme Court. When introducing John Roberts and Samuel Alito, President Bush argued that Roberts and Alito deserved bipartisan support because they would "interpret the Constitution and the laws faithfully and fairly, to protect the constitutional rights of all Americans," and they would not "impose their preferences or priorities on the people." The nominees similarly promised to be "umpires" without "any agenda" or "any preferred outcome in any particular case."

These statements at the time seemed hard to reconcile with facts in the record. On the campaign trail, President Bush had rallied his base with promises to nominate "strict constructionists" to the Supreme Court in the mold of Antonin Scalia and Clarence Thomas. Roberts, meanwhile, had been part of what his former colleague Bruce Fein called a "band of ideological brothers" who argued for dramatic changes in the law during the Reagan administration. Alito had submitted a 1985 job application detailing his "disagreement with Warren Court opinions" and his desire to "help advance legal positions [of the Reagan administration] in which I personally believe very strongly." Indeed, both Roberts and Alito spent their early careers serving the executive branch of ideologically-driven administrations rather than gaining the kind of real world experience brought to the Court by justices such as the one Alito replaced, Sandra Day O'Connor.

The Senate and the American people by and large believed the promises made by Bush, Roberts, and Alito and discounted the discordant facts in the record. Both judges were confirmed with bipartisan support. One Senator, before voting for the confirmation of Chief Justice Roberts, said: "Today I will vote my hopes and not my fears."

Sadly, after nearly two terms together on the Supreme Court, it is clear that the Senate's fears about Roberts and Alito are being realized, their hopes dashed. Last term, Roberts and Alito voted together in 88 percent of non-unanimous cases—more than any other two justices. So far this term, Roberts and Alito have voted together in 18 of the 20 cases that have divided the Court by five to four margins. Together with Justices Thomas and Scalia, Alito and Roberts have formed a solid conservative bloc of four justices in every major case, splitting the court along ideological lines.

In reaching a conservative political outcome in these cases, Justices Roberts and Alito have run roughshod over many of the critical rule of law principles that limit the role politics can play in judicial decision-making, including respect for equal access to the courts, respect for the democratic process, and respect for precedent.

The Supreme Court's brace of rulings today are thoroughly emblematic of the two justice's disrespect for all three legal principles. In *Leegin Creative Leather Products v. PSKS*, Roberts and Alito voted to overturn a nearly century-old decision preventing manufacturers from setting a minimum price retailers may charge for their products.

The decision by Alito and Roberts to overturn this long-established precedent is particularly remarkable because the case involves interpretation of a statute. The Court is particularly committed to *stare decisis* in statutory cases because Congress can amend a statute if it thinks the Court has erred in its interpretation. This disregard for precedent may be a historic first. Breyer asserts in dissent: "I am not aware of any case in which this Court has overturned so well-established a statutory precedent."

Chief Justice Roberts' opinion, joined by Alito in the Louisville and Seattle race cases—*Parents Involved in Community Schools v. Seattle School District No. 1* and *Meredith v. Jefferson County Board of Education*—so perfectly illustrates the rule-of-law concerns raised by this term's opinion that it warrants its own discussion.

As an initial matter, the opinion vividly contradicts Roberts professed preference for crafting "narrow" opinions that achieve as much consensus as possible on the Court. There were five votes on the Court for the proposition that the Seattle and Louisville plans did not meet the Court's strict scrutiny test for race-conscious classifications. Roberts' opinion could have ended with this conclusion.

Instead, Roberts wrote two additional sections, joined only by Alito, Scalia, and Thomas, which fully equate race-conscious efforts to promote integration with racial segregation and root this conclusion in the Supreme Court's landmark ruling in *Brown v. Board of Education*. There is, in Stevens' words, a "cruel irony" in this use of the *Brown* opinion, and these deeply divisive conclusions were totally unnecessary for the resolution of the case.

As Kennedy argues quite forcefully in a separate opinion, Roberts "is too dismissive of the legitimate interests government has in ensuring all people have equal opportunity regardless of their race." This is just one of many rule-of-law concerns highlighted by Roberts' opinion in the Seattle and Louisville cases:

- Roberts and Alito show an alarming lack of respect for precedent. As Breyer argues persuasively in dissent, Roberts' opinion refuses to follow a "longstanding and unbroken line of legal authority tells us that the Equal Protection Clause permits local school boards to use race-conscious criteria to achieve positive race-related goals, even when the Constitution does not compel it."
- Roberts and Alito fail to respect the democratic process. The plurality portions of their opinion, in particular, would overturn decisions made by elected officials in communities in communities across the country. As Breyer puts it in dissent, the "Constitution allows democratically elected school boards to make up their own minds as to how best to include people of all races in one America."
- Roberts and Alito disregard constitutional history. Some conservatives, notably Scalia and Thomas, purport to be

bound by the original understanding or the Constitution. But there is no evidence that anyone alive at the time the 14th Amendment was passed thought it would ban race-conscious efforts to promote integrated schools. Indeed, as Breyer demonstrates, historical research shows that the generation of Americans who enacted the Equal Protection Clause also used race-conscious measures to promote school integration. Roberts' opinion ignores this constitutional history.

The opinions joined by Roberts and Alito are by no means isolated cases. Consider the following:

Respect for Precedent

Following a doctrine known as *stare decisis*, Latin for "let it stand," the Supreme Court generally builds off its prior rulings rather than overruling them. Yet in several recent cases, Alito and Roberts have treated this doctrine, and the Court's earlier rulings, with an alarming lack of respect.

Bowles v. Russell: Alito and Roberts voted to overrule two long-standing Supreme Court rulings even though no one in the case had filed a brief asking the Court to overrule these cases.

Gonzales v. Carhart: Roberts and Alito upheld a federal abortion ban that contains no exception for the health of a woman even though the law was nearly identical to the law struck down by the Court only seven years earlier in *Stenberg v. Carhart*. As Justice Ginsburg noted in dissent, the opinion joined by Alito and Roberts "is hardly faithful to our earlier invocations of 'the rule of law' and the 'principles of *stare decisis*.'"

FEC v. Wisconsin Right to Life: Roberts and Alito voted to dramatically curtail restrictions on "sham issue ads," regulated by the Bipartisan Campaign Reform Act. While Roberts and Alito purport not to overrule the Supreme Court's 2003 ruling in *McConnell v. FEC*, the other seven justices all agreed that their opinion "effectively overrules *McConnell* without saying so." In Justice Scalia's words: "[t]his faux judicial restraint is judicial obfuscation."

National Association of Home Builders v. Defenders of Wildlife: Roberts and Alito ruled that Section 7 of the Endangered Species Act, which requires that all federal agencies "shall" insure that their actions do not jeopardize endangered species, does not apply to nondiscretionary federal actions. This ruling contradicts the Court's earlier ruling in *TVA v. Hill*, which explained that Section 7 "admits of no exception." As Justice Stevens notes in dissent, this ruling "turns its back on our decision in *Hill* and places a great number of endangered species in jeopardy."

Hein v. Freedom from Religion: Roberts and Alito threw out a lawsuit challenging President Bush's Faith-Based Initiative, ruling that taxpayers had no "standing" to challenge the program, notwithstanding the Court's 1968 ruling in *Flast v. Cohen* that found taxpayer standing in a very similar context. Justice Souter, in dissent, asserts that "a search of [the Alito/Roberts plurality] opinion for a suggestion that these taxpayers have any less stake in the outcome than the taxpayers in *Flast* will come up empty: the plurality makes no such finding, nor could it." Justice Scalia is even more scathing, stating in a concurrence that "laying just claim to be honoring *stare decisis* requires more than beating *Flast* to a pulp and then sending it out to the lower courts weakened, denigrated, more incomprehensible than ever, and yet somehow technically alive."

Respect for the Democratic Process

Absent clear constitutional mandates, unelected judges should generally defer to the decisions on complex policy questions made by Congress—the branch of our federal government most representative of the will of the people. In many cases over the last two terms, Roberts and Alito have voted in ways that show a disturbing lack of deference, if not outright hostility, to the laws passed by Congress.

FEC v. Wisconsin Right to Life: Roberts and Alito effectively overturned the reasoned judgment of a bipartisan majority in

Congress that "sham issue ads" were corrupting the nations' political process.

Ledbetter v. Goodyear: Alito and Roberts ignored both the broad remedial mandate of Title VII of the Civil Rights Act of 1964 and the intent of Congress in the Civil Rights Act of 1991 in ruling that a victim of workplace discrimination could not sue her employer even when intentional past discrimination continued to result in current disparities in pay.

Rapanos v. US: Alito and Roberts joined a plurality ruling that sought to dramatically limit the reach of the Clean Water Act, leaving vast amounts of the waters and wetlands currently protected by the Act unprotected. Justice Kennedy described the opinion joined by Alito and Roberts as "unduly dismissive of the interests asserted by the United States in these cases." Justice Stevens was blunter, stating that the opinion joined by Roberts and Alito displayed "antagonism to environmentalism."

Massachusetts v. EPA: Roberts and Alito voted in dissent to deny the EPA authority under the Clean Air Act to address global warming pollution—even though the Act itself called carbon dioxide a pollutant. Justice Stevens, writing for the Court's majority, explained that this interpretation was flatly inconsistent with the text of the Act.

Arlington Cent. Sch. Dist. v. Murphy: Roberts and Alito voted that parents who successfully challenge their local school board for violating the mandates of the Individuals with Disabilities Education Act should not recover the costs of retaining the expert witnesses necessary to prevail in such suits—even though Congress clearly intended that such costs be recoverable.

National Association of Homebuilders v. Defenders of Wildlife: Alito and Roberts refused to follow the clear mandate from Congress that every federal agency should consider the impact of each of its actions on the continued survival of endangered species.

Respect for Equal Access to Courts

Roberts told the Senate that he would be an umpire, just calling balls and strikes. But Alito and Roberts have frequently ruled in ways that have shut the courthouse doors, effectively preventing a game from even beginning. Most disturbingly, court-access rulings by Roberts and Alito seem designed mainly to exclude particular types of litigants, such as victims of discrimination and criminal defendants, who have long been disfavored by political conservatives. These rulings disrespect the edict of the great Chief Justice Marshall in *Marbury v. Madison*, which holds: "[the very essence of civil liberty certainly consists in the right of every individual to claim the protection of the laws, whenever he receives an injury. One of the first duties of government is to afford that protection."

Bowles vs. Russell: Roberts and Alito voted to deny an appeal of a district court ruling because the appeal was filed two days late—even though the untimely filing was caused by the erroneous instructions given Bowles in an order issued by a federal district judge.

Schriro v. Landrigan: Alito and Roberts refused to order a hearing on a claim of ineffective assistance of counsel in a death penalty case, finding that the petitioner waived his right to present mitigating evidence. In dissent, Justice Stevens observed that the outcome could "only be explained by [the majority's] increasingly familiar effort to guard the floodgates of litigation." But as Stevens pointedly notes, "doing justice does not always cause the heavens to fall."

Ledbetter v. Goodyear: Alito and Roberts threw out a Title VII suit even though a jury found Ms. Ledbetter was the victim of intentional sex discrimination and that, as a result, she was receiving less money in each paycheck than men in similar positions and with similar seniority. Under the rule they imposed, a victim of discrimination is required to file a complaint even before he or she is aware that a discriminatory decision has been made—or be barred from court forever.

Hein v. Freedom for Religion: Roberts and Alito voted to close the Court's doors on taxpayers, arguing that the President's Faith-Based Initiative promoted religious organizations in violation of the Constitution's Establishment Clause.

In short, the Roberts and Alito on the Supreme Court are nothing like the Roberts and Alito in testimony before Congress and in public appearances before the American people prior to their confirmation by the Senate to the nation's highest bench. This politicization of the Supreme Court by President Bush is dangerous to the rule of law and precedent, equal rights before the law, and our nation's democratic principles.

4

Chief Justice Roberts Has Led by Moderate Institutionalism

Robin Effron

Robin Effron is a professor of law at Brooklyn Law School, where she teaches civil procedure, litigation, and international business law. She previously served as a Bigelow Fellow and Lecturer in Law at the University of Chicago Law School.

Supreme Court Chief Justice John Roberts has been an example of judicial moderation and institutional restraint. Known as a staunch conservative prior to his nomination in 2005, Chief Justice Roberts has since adopted a cautious judicial philosophy. In both his writings and in public statements, he often seems more concerned with maintaining the institutional integrity of the court than he is with advancing any distinct ideology. The viewpoint also examines how Chief Justice Roberts's influence on the court has impacted litigant strategy in various instances.

Centrists and progressives pinned their hopes for ideological balance on Chief Justice John Roberts' desire to preserve the Court's image as an apolitical institution. But explicit calls for the Court to consider institutional integrity are themselves contributing to its increased politicization.

This time last year, the American public waited anxiously to see if Brett Kavanaugh would become the newest US Supreme Court justice. The confirmation was an important one, because supporters and detractors alike assumed that President Donald Trump's newest pick would reshape the ideological composition of the Court. With the addition of a new conservative justice, some liberals have been looking to Chief Justice John Roberts as the possible new centrist or "swing vote" on the Court. Although Justice Roberts is generally a reliably conservative voice, commentators point to a gentle leftward drift and a few key votes as examples of his moderation, such as his majority opinion upholding the Affordable Care Act.

Justice Roberts, the argument goes, might have genuine conservative priors. But he is also deeply committed to protecting the institution of the Supreme Court itself and insulating it from the charge that it has just become a third political branch of the federal government. For anyone worried about the future of abortion access, LGBT rights, affirmative action, or pushback against the executive excesses of the Trump presidency, this belief isn't a strain. Justice Roberts seems, at worst, committed to a strategy of incremental change rather than abrupt action, such as a vote to completely overturn *Roe v. Wade*. More hopeful observers offer soothing reassurances that Roberts' long-term interest in the institution of the Supreme Court will be a powerful moderating influence, both in the votes he casts and in the opinions he writes.

Hot-Button Cases

Even if this is true, the "institutional integrity" line of thinking works only if we assume that the most important issues appear in the highest-profile cases. A few key votes on hot-button cases might give the Roberts Court cover to move further rightward on lesser-known issues, or cases involving technical and complex issues that are not easily reduced to Twitter-friendly sound bites. We can expect the pro-business bent of the Court to continue to move further and further right. And in one key subset of cases, the Roberts Court can, with minimal attention and outcry from the general public, push the Court further right with serious consequences for decades to come.

These cases come from the rather dull-sounding area of law called civil procedure. Although these issues may seem boring, a series of carefully picked and well-timed decisions could allow the Court to significantly narrow Americans' access to justice without ever confronting the politically charged issues that dominate the news cycle. The Court has already narrowed consumers' and employees' rights to bring collective actions in arbitration, to file efficient class actions in a single court for defective products, or to sue foreign manufacturers for dangerous products without traveling to a distant American or even foreign forum. More ominously, the Court has been steadily curtailing plaintiffs' abilities to sue government officials for constitutional violations.

The Supreme Court exercises discretionary control over its docket, and it can easily pick procedural cases that seem distant from the everyday lives and concerns of most Americans—perhaps a dispute about where one can sue a railway, or the question of whether a construction company can force a court to transfer a case from one state to another. But no one should be fooled by the humdrum dispute and the dry complexities of the procedural law at issue. These cases form the backbone of our ability to vindicate important public and private rights in court, and a conservative Court could bury a sharp rightward turn in the procedural weeds.

Weaponizing Institutional Integrity

Amid all the handicapping of the newly composed Supreme Court is another new development. It's true that Justice Roberts is known for caring deeply about the institutional integrity of the Supreme Court, and many centrists and progressives pinned their hopes for ideological balance on his apparent desire to preserve the Court's image as an apolitical institution. But paradoxically, explicit calls for the Court to consider institutional integrity are themselves contributing to the increased politicization of the Court. Indeed, a few cases from last term show that appealing to

Justice Roberts' sense of institutional integrity can be effective. But more recent events show that the "institutional integrity" card can be weaponized.

Litigants and other interested parties have good reason to believe that strategies that emphasize judicial integrity and impartiality may be persuasive. Sometimes Justice Roberts speaks directly about the importance of an apolitical judiciary, such as when he rebuked President Trump for complaining about a decision by an "Obama judge" that blocked the administration's efforts to restrict asylum. Other decisions show his ability to use procedural tools to delay or avoid politically sensitive decisions, such as his opinion in the census citizenship question case, *Department of Commerce v. New York*, in which he wrote that a citizenship question itself is not unconstitutional, but that the Commerce Department had provided only pretextual reasons for its inclusion; or his decision to join with the Court's four liberal justices in granting a stay of the enforcement of a Louisiana anti-abortion law, *June Medical Services v. Gee*, while the parties petitioned the Court for certiorari.

It should be no surprise, then, that some parties and other groups have begun to make explicit institutional integrity arguments to the Court. Consider the recent partisan spat between Senate Democrats and Republicans surrounding an upcoming Second Amendment case pending before the Supreme Court, *New York State Rifle & Pistol Association v. City of New York, New York*. The case concerns a restriction that New York City passed on transporting licensed handguns outside the home. Gun rights advocates challenged the restriction in federal court and lost in the district court and before the Second Circuit. Nevertheless, when the Supreme Court granted certiorari to hear the challenge to this case, New York City officials changed the regulation to permit the challenged activity. They then moved to dismiss the Supreme Court petition as moot.

Inevitable End Point

Here is where things really started to get political. In mid-August, a group of Democratic US senators filed an amicus brief arguing in favor of the mootness dismissal. Their brief made a direct connection between mootness—a superficially arcane and apolitical legal doctrine—and the institutional integrity of the Supreme Court. They argued that a decision to hear the case, despite the fact that the petitioners were no longer aggrieved by an existing regulation, would reveal a political bias toward an aggressively conservative interpretation of the Second Amendment. Senate Republicans recently issued a strong rebuke to this filing, accusing the Democrats of playing politics. Although the Republicans did not take a formal stance on the issue of mootness, they strongly intimated that ruling in New York City's favor on the mootness issue would be a capitulation to the Democrats' political interests and "capture" of the Supreme Court, claiming that the Democrats had "openly threatened the Court with political retribution." Perhaps this is the inevitable end point of the obsession with institutional integrity. When the perceived defining feature of a "swing vote" or "centrist judge" is a commitment to the institution and its attendant procedures, it is only a matter of time before institutional integrity itself is politicized. Although it is certainly nothing new to see academics tussle over these questions, or to see these issues discussed as explanatory commentary on the Court's cases and decisions, Justice Roberts may find that by centering the importance of an image of judicial independence, he has only encouraged the politicization of that very issue.

Predicting what Justice Roberts will do this term with respect to issues of institutional integrity is difficult. But it's safe to say that litigants and commentators will only increase vocal and direct appeals about how each case or issue will affect the Court as an institution. In the end, this might not be a terrible outcome. If the Court is, in fact, grounding some aspects of its decision making and reasoning in concerns about institutional integrity, litigants and the public at large should have the opportunity to participate in that dialogue. It will be up to Justice Roberts to ensure that such debates are an enhancement rather than a distraction, and that the issue of institutional integrity does not take on such a life of its own that it swallows the merits' questions whole.

The good news is, we still have a system designed for balanced discourse. Those who care about access to justice can start raising the profile of potential Supreme Court cases that would make it harder for Americans to vindicate their rights in court. Let Justice Roberts know that the integrity of the Court depends as much on access to justice as it does on maintaining political balance. Better yet, most of the doors to our court system are open and shut by Congress and rule makers, not by the Constitution. We need to stop relying on courts to save our access to justice, and turn instead to Congress, procedural rule makers, and other legislative bodies to pass legislation that keeps Americans' abilities to vindicate their rights in state and federal court from disappearing into a morass of "mere technicalities."

5

The Supreme Court Has a Mixed Record of Willingness to Stand Up to the Political Process

Erwin Chemerinsky

Erwin Chemerinsky is the current dean of the University of California, Berkeley School of Law. Previously he held positions on the faculty at the University of California–Irvine and Duke University.

In this viewpoint, the author asks whether the Supreme Court is meeting its institutional responsibility to provide a constitutional check on the political process. He looks specifically at the recent Rucho v. Common Cause *case from North Carolina, which challenged the constitutionality of "gerrymandered" congressional districts (i.e., districts that are drawn specifically to provide electoral advantage to the party in power). Although the majority opinion acknowledged that such tactics are "incompatible with democratic principles," the court declined to intervene. The author argues that the court's inaction on this case represents an abdication of authority by the judiciary.*

The most important role of the federal judiciary, including the Supreme Court, is to check the political process by enforcing the constitution.

At times, the court has performed this role admirably, as it did when it brought an end to the laws that created apartheid

"The Supreme Court Is Supposed to Be a Check on the Political Process. Is It Still?" by Erwin Chemerinsky, Guardian News & Media Limited, June 27, 2019. Reprinted by permission.

and required legal segregation of the races. At other times, the court has failed miserably—for example in continually upholding slavery before the civil war, and in allowing the government to intern 110,000 Japanese-Americans during the Second World War.

As the Supreme Court finished its term on Thursday, it once again had a mixed record of being willing to stand up to the political process.

Most importantly, the court said federal courts cannot hear challenges to partisan gerrymandering. Political gerrymandering is when the political party that controls a legislature draws election districts to maximize safe seats for that party. For example, in one of the cases before the court, the Republican-controlled North Carolina legislature drew congressional districts with the explicit goal of ensuring that Republicans won 10 of 13 seats in the House of Representatives.

North Carolina is basically a purple state, having gone for Obama in 2008, Romney in 2012, and Trump in 2016, always by very close margins. In 2016, Democrats and Republicans received almost exactly the same number of votes across the state for congressional seats, but the gerrymandering succeeded and Republicans took 10 of 13 seats, as planned.

A federal court ruled that this kind of gerrymandering violates the First Amendment by discriminating against people because of their political affiliation. It is unconstitutional, the court argued, to deny equal protection by effectively diluting people's votes. It undermines the democratic process: no longer do voters choose their elected officials; elected officials now choose their voters.

In its decision, the Supreme Court's majority acknowledged this, calling partisan gerrymandering "incompatible with democratic principles."

The majority opinion dodged responsibility, however, by arguing that challenges to partisan gerrymandering are "political questions" that cannot be heard by the federal courts. The decision was 5–4, split along ideological lines, with the majority opinion written by Chief Justice John Roberts.

The court said there aren't any clear standards for when gerrymandering violates the constitution. But leaving this problem to be solved in the political process makes no sense: legislators who benefit from partisan gerrymandering are obviously not going to change the process. The court effectively put the fox in charge of the hen house.

The majority decision is also anti-historical: the court can—and does—create legal standards, as it has in so many other areas, for when gerrymandering goes too far and violates the constitution.

The court did exactly this in the 1960s, when it held that malapportionment of state legislatures violated the constitution. Prior to that, many state legislatures were badly malapportioned—there might be one district with 50,000 people and another with 250,000. Those in the latter district were obviously disadvantaged by the dilution of their political power.

The court declared this unconstitutional and fashioned as a remedy the principle "one person–one vote," meaning that legislative districts must be about the same size in population. Chief Justice Earl Warren later remarked that of all the decisions during his tenure on the court, he was most proud of the cases about malapportionment because the political process would not work to correct the problem; legislators who benefited from the practice were not about to change it.

The court should have dealt with partisan gerrymandering the same way. It chose not to. In her dissent, Justice Elena Kagan powerfully explained what was wrong with the majority's decision:

> *For the first time ever, this court refuses to remedy a constitutional violation because it thinks the task beyond judicial capabilities. And not just any constitutional violation. The partisan gerrymanders in these cases deprived citizens of the most fundamental of their constitutional rights: the rights to participate equally in the political process, to join with others to advance political beliefs, and to choose their political representatives. In so doing, the partisan gerrymanders here debased and dishonored*

our democracy, turning upside-down the core American idea that
all governmental power derives from the people.

In the other major ruling of the day, the court, at least for now, stood up to the Trump administration and said that it must give a legitimate reason for asking on the 2020 census form whether a person is a citizen.

The constitution requires a regular census every decade to ensure an accurate "enumeration" of the people. Being as accurate as possible in the count is crucial because seats in the House of Representatives are allocated based on the census and many federal programs apportion money based on it as well.

The commerce department, which administers the census, added a question about whether a person is a citizen for the 2020 census. A question on citizenship was included on census forms from 1820 until 1950, while some households received forms that contained the question between 1960 and 2000. But the census form sent to all households has not included it in almost 70 years.

Contrary to the claims of Republicans, it is clear that asking whether a person is a citizen will make the census less accurate, not more: undocumented immigrants and even documented citizens would be much less likely to participate in the census.

In earlier decisions, federal district courts ruled against the Trump administration. They said that decisions of administrative agencies like the census bureau must have a reasonable basis, and there is no reasonable justification for including the question on citizenship.

The Trump administration initially gave no reason for the proposed change—then claimed it was to aid in the enforcement of the federal Voting Rights Act of 1965. But there is no evidence that enforcement of that Act for the past 54 years has been hindered in any way by the absence of this question on the census. Indeed, there is no evidence from the justice department that asking this question on the census would do anything to help enforce voting rights.

As Justice Breyer—joined by the court's other three liberal justices—argued, the Supreme Court should have affirmed the lower court's ruling and struck down the question about citizenship as arbitrary and capricious and thus in violation of federal law. But the five conservative justices refused, and instead sent the case back to the lower courts to give the Trump administration another chance to justify its case.

With a president who pushes constitutional boundaries like none other in American history, it is crucial the Supreme Court perform its constitutional duty as a check and balance on the political process. Unfortunately, it is not clear that it will.

6

Roe v. Wade and the Politics of Abortion Rights

USHistory.org

USHistory.org is an online resource published by the Independence Hall Association (IHA), a Pennsylvania-based nonprofit dedicated to educating the public about topics in American history.

This viewpoint looks at the impact of abortion rights, one of the most explosive and controversial issues in American politics over the past several decades, and especially since the 1973 Supreme Court decision Roe v. Wade. *Liberals tend to believe that the* Roe *decision established critically important rights for women to take control of their own health care. Conservatives tend to focus on the morality of abortion (often framed in terms of Christian doctrine) and usually regard the* Roe *decision as an example of judicial overreach. The tension between these perspectives has been one of the main threads in American politics for nearly half a century.*

N o topic related to the feminist movement has aroused such passion and controversy as much as the right to an abortion. In the 1960s, there was no federal law regulating abortions, and many states had banned the practice entirely, except when the life of the mother was endangered.

Women's groups argued that illegality led many women to seek black market abortions by unlicensed physicians or to perform the procedure on themselves. As a result, several states such as

"57d. *Roe v. Wade* and Its Impact," UShistory.org. Reprinted by permission.

California and New York began to legitimize abortions. With no definitive ruling from the federal government, women's groups sought the opinion of the United States Supreme Court.

The battle began in Texas, which outlawed any type of abortion unless a doctor determined that the mother's life was in danger. The anonymous Jane Roe challenged the Texas law, and the case slowly made its way to the highest court in the land.

After two years of hearing evidence, the Court invalidated the Texas law by a 7-2 vote. Using the same reasoning as the *Griswold v. Connecticut* decision, the majority of the justices maintained that a right to privacy was implied by the Ninth and Fourteenth Amendments. No state could restrict abortions during the first three months, or trimester, of a pregnancy.

States were permitted to adopt restrictive laws in accordance with respecting the mother's health during the second trimester. The practice could be banned outright during the third trimester. Any state law that conflicted with this ruling was automatically overturned.

Women's groups were ecstatic. But immediately an opposition emerged. The Roman Catholic Church had long criticized abortion as a form of infanticide. Many fundamentalist Protestant ministers joined the outcry. The National Right to Life Committee formed with the explicit goal of reversing *Roe v. Wade*.

The issue is fundamentally thorny because it involves basic faiths. Those who believe life begins at conception feel that the unborn child deserves the same legal protections as an adult. Ending such a life is equivalent to murder to those who subscribe to this belief. Others argue that life begins at birth, and that laws restricting abortion interfere with the right of a woman to decide what is in her own best interests. Opponents of abortion use the label "Pro-Life" to define their cause. Supporters of *Roe v. Wade* identify themselves as "Pro-Choice."

Since 1973, the battle has raged. Pro-life groups began to lobby their Senators and Representatives to propose a Right-to-Life Amendment to the Constitution. Although introduced in

Congress, the measure has never received the necessary support. Pro-choice groups such as the National Abortion Rights Action League fear that a slow erosion of abortion rights has taken place since *Roe v. Wade*.

The Hyde Amendment of 1976 prohibits the use of federal Medicaid funds to be used for abortions. Later Court decisions such as *Planned Parenthood v. Casey* (1992) have upheld the right of states to impose waiting periods and parental notification requirements. President George Bush imposed a "gag rule" that prohibited workers in federally funded clinics from even mentioning abortion as an option with their patients. Bill Clinton promptly ended the gag rule in 1993.

Planned Parenthood clinics have become local battlegrounds over the abortion controversy. Since Planned Parenthood prides itself in providing safe, inexpensive abortions, protesters regularly picket outside their offices. Several Planned Parenthood sites have even been bombed by antiabortion extremists.

The fate of *Roe v. Wade* continues to lie with the Supreme Court. Although every ruling since 1973 upheld the decision, the composition of the Court changes with every retirement. Activists on each side demand a "litmus test" for any justice named to the federal courts. Republicans have tended to appoint pro-life judges, and Democrats have selected pro-choice nominees.

At the dawn of the 21st century, the battle remains as fierce as ever.

7

Questioning the Stability of the *Roe v. Wade* Precedent

Julie Rovner

Julie Rovner is an American journalist whose work focuses on health care policy. She is the Robin Toner Distinguished Fellow and chief Washington correspondent for Kaiser Health News. She also reports for National Public Radio, National Journal's CongressDaily, and Congressional Quarterly.

This short viewpoint examines the impact and current standing of the legal precedent established by the Roe v. Wade *decision in 1973. The author—one of the top health policy journalists in the US—identifies moments over the past several decades in which the decision appeared vulnerable to challenge, particularly the recent* June Medical Services v. Gee *case in Louisiana. The author suggests that it may be useful from a health policy perspective to consider the legal right to abortion as separate from real access to abortion services.*

Jan. 22 marks the 47th anniversary of *Roe v. Wade*, the landmark court case that legalized abortion nationwide. People on both sides of the furious debate say this could be the year when everything changes.

In March, the US Supreme Court will hear its first abortion case since Justice Brett Kavanaugh replaced Anthony Kennedy,

"*Roe v. Wade*: Settled Law or Bad Precedent? States Prep for an Overturn," by Julie Rovner, NPR, January 21, 2020. Reprinted by permission.

who had been the swing vote on abortion cases. A decision is expected by summer.

The case, *June Medical Services v. Gee*, challenges a Louisiana law that requires doctors who perform abortions to have admitting privileges at a nearby hospital. It's a reprise of a case decided in 2016, when a five-vote majority (including Kennedy's) struck down a similar Texas law in *Whole Woman's Health v. Hellerstedt*.

On Jan. 2, more than 200 Republican members of the House and Senate filed a brief in the *Gee* case urging the justices to use it to overturn *Roe* once and for all. "Forty-six years after *Roe* was decided, it remains a radically unsettled precedent," the brief said. And the 1992 case that reiterated a curtailed right to abortion, *Planned Parenthood of Southeastern Pennsylvania v. Casey*, did not help, the members argued. "*Casey* clearly did not settle the abortion issue, and it is time for the Court to take it up again."

But many legal scholars say the court is far more likely to rule narrowly in the case than to use it to overturn *Roe* and/or *Casey*, because that's what the Supreme Court tends to do.

Still, even if the court does not overturn *Roe*, it might do something that could hasten *Roe*'s demise: Uphold the Louisiana law by ruling that abortion providers cannot sue on behalf of their patients, something the state of Louisiana is urging it to do. That would make it much more difficult to challenge state abortion restrictions because only women seeking abortions would be able to challenge those laws in court. Many pregnant women seeking abortions don't want to go to the additional trouble of becoming part of a highly public lawsuit that could take years.

"That would be a bigger deal" than finding some other legal justification to uphold Louisiana's law, says Mary Ziegler, a law professor at Florida State University who has written several books on abortion and abortion law.

It's part and parcel of an anti-abortion strategy: Make abortion more difficult to obtain even where it is technically legal.

"A right is certainly important," says Elisabeth Smith of the Center for Reproductive Rights, an abortion-rights legal advocacy group. "But if you cannot access abortion care, that right is meaningless."

Since 2004, the group has periodically looked at what would happen to abortion laws in states if the Supreme Court were to reverse its conclusion that abortion, at least in some cases, is a right guaranteed by the US Constitution. In its original report, titled "What If Roe Fell," and again in 2007 and 2017, the center assessed the likely legal status of abortion in the states, because in the absence of *Roe*, abortion's legality would be determined by state lawmakers or state constitutions.

But in its 2019 version of "What If Roe Fell," the group took a slightly different tack. This latest iteration looked at likely legality, but also at the relative availability of the procedure. The report concludes that if the Supreme Court eliminates federal protections for abortion, the procedure is likely to be immediately prohibited in 24 states and remain legal and generally available in 21. The five other states and the District of Columbia have not established a right to abortion.

Even with *Roe* still standing, Smith says, some states, such as Mississippi and Missouri, are already abortion "deserts," where the procedure is all but unavailable.

Nonetheless, "the situation would be much worse if the federal right is limited or overturned," she says. In fact, some states are "havens" that have made abortions easier to obtain. For now, "abortion is still legal. Every state has at least one abortion clinic," Smith adds.

This is far from the first time it appeared *Roe* was teetering on the brink. In 1992, after Justice Clarence Thomas replaced Thurgood Marshall, one of the original seven justices in the majority in *Roe*, the country braced for an overturn. It did not happen.

In 2005, when Justice Sandra Day O'Connor, a swing vote on abortion, retired and was replaced by Justice Samuel Alito, the alarms were raised again. And the overturn of *Roe v. Wade* did not happen. Then in 2018, when Kennedy—O'Connor's successor as the abortion swing vote—retired and was replaced by Kavanaugh, the bells rang once more.

The Louisiana case is the first chance for what would appear to be a clear five-vote anti-abortion majority to rule.

Ziegler, the Florida State law professor, warns that overturning *Roe* would not end the fight.

"If this goes back to the states, it's going to continue indefinitely," Ziegler says. "The endpoint for people who oppose abortion is not just allowing states to decide."

In other words, if you think the abortion issue is inflammatory now, just wait and see what happens if *Roe* is gone.

8

To Insulate the Supreme Court from Politics, Overturn *Roe v. Wade*

Steven H. Aden

Steven H. Aden is a conservative lawyer who currently serves as chief legal officer and general counsel at Americans United for Life. He has written extensively on "sanctity of life" issues and constitutional jurisprudence.

This viewpoint exemplifies the modern conservative perspective on constitutional jurisprudence. For many conservatives, the current politicization of the Supreme Court can be traced directly to the 1973 Roe v. Wade *decision. Conservatives tend to regard* Roe v. Wade *as an example of undemocratic judicial overreach on an issue of intense emotional and religious importance to many conservative voters. The author argues that much of the partisan warfare over Supreme Court appointments in recent decades emerges directly from political resentment on this point.*

We must never forget that it is a constitution we are expounding," cautioned John Marshall, one of the first Chief Justices of the US Supreme Court. Marshall, speaking almost exactly two hundred years ago for the Court in *McCulloch v. Maryland*, had foresight. Forgetting what a constitution is, and what that implies for expounding it, is the central political problem of our day. Constitution Day, September 17th, the date on which

"Politics and the Supreme Court," by Steven H. Aden, *National Review*, September 17, 2019. Reprinted by permission.

the Framers of the Constitution signed the nation's charter into law, is an opportunity to remember—and take warning.

Judicial independence is the crowning glory of the American constitutional system, and the Supreme Court's singular commitment to the Constitution and laws of the Republic—with its concomitant determination to avoid political entanglements—is the brightest jewel in that crown. To those who questioned whether a federal court system was appropriate in a nation of limited central government, Alexander Hamilton famously defended the co-equal role of the federal judiciary in Federalist 78 by contending that the judicial branch would "always be the least dangerous to the political rights of the Constitution," because it would be least capable of imposing its will on the other branches and the People.

Federal courts have no army at their command, no police force to enforce their decrees. The judiciary, Hamilton said, has "neither force nor will, but merely judgment." The power of the Federal Marshal's Office may cow an individual litigant into compliance with a court's injunctive order, but the broader authority enjoyed by the Supreme Court and the federal courts of appeals can only depend on respect for the Rule of Law and the courts' unique place in upholding that principle. The Rule of Law doesn't just depend upon respect for the courts—it is respect for the courts. Federal judges—alone among federal officials—have lifetime tenure in their jobs to insulate themselves from pressures that would inevitably arise from the need to stand for election or to secure political appointment or re-appointment.

For this reason, the Supreme Court ought to be respected in its inurement from the political forces that—by constitutional design—perpetually crash like storm waves against the Congress and the president. Once the Justices begin to decide disputes with an eye toward the impact their decisions may have on the country's often-heated heated political discourse, not only the trust reposed on the judicial system by litigants, but even more importantly the meaning of the law itself—of federal statutes and constitutional provisions—is subject to distortion for political ends.

That's why a "friend of the Court" brief five US Senators filed recently with the Supreme Court should unsettle anyone who values the Court's constitutionally safeguarded independence. "The Supreme Court is not well. And the people know it," Senator Sheldon Whitehouse of Rhode Island and his collaborators told the Court in a case involving the scope of the Second Amendment's "right to bear arms." "Perhaps the Court can heal itself before the public demands it be 'restructured in order to reduce the influence of politics.'" The brief can't be taken as anything but a crudely-veiled warning that if the Justices fail to reach the "right" result, the US Senate would consider extreme political retribution—such as "packing the Court" with additional "right-thinking" jurists, as some threatened to do to protect President Franklin Roosevelt's New Deal programs. Thankfully, fifty-three senators penned a powerful reply to the "Gang of Five," reminding the Justices that "Judicial independence is not negotiable…. Our constitutional republic depends on an independent judiciary ruling impartially on the basis of what the law says."

A ready handful of hot topics come up when the discussion turns to "political" questions the Supreme Court faces from time to time: electoral gerrymandering, the "right to bear arms," *Bush v. Gore*, and the like. But abortion stands alone as the most potently corrosive force in modern constitutional jurisprudence. The demand for abortion distorts every doctrine of constitutional law it touches, from the Article III requirement for constitutional standing and the Fourteenth Amendment right of due process, to the First Amendment free speech rights of pro-life advocates and the free exercise rights of pro-life doctors, nurses and pharmacists. Beginning with *Roe* in 1973, the rush by activist judges to ignore medical science, history, and judicial precedent in order to erect a high wall against virtually every reasonable restriction on abortion has no parallel in American law, save for the country's shameful denial of the humanity and dignity of persons for their racial heritage. Members of the Supreme Court have described judicial review in abortion cases as an "ad hoc nullification machine" for laws restricting abortion, and charged that abortion has worked "a major distortion in the Court's constitutional jurisprudence."

Clearly, *Roe* needs to go. But there is apparently at least a three-Justice bloc—Chief Justice John Roberts, Samuel Alito, and Brett Kavanaugh—that believes that "special justification," more than mere constitutional error, is required to overturn precedent. Likewise, many have suggested that the Court would or should wait for more than a bare one-member majority to overturn *Roe*. But neither a "special justification" nor a felt need on the part of the Court's conservatives to avoid a narrow and vociferous public split made any difference in 2010 in *Citizens United v. FEC*, in last year's decision in *Janus v. AFSCME* (no forced subsidization of public sector unions), or this year in *Franchise Tax Board v. Hyatt* (states can't be sued in courts of other states), all 5-4 decisions. Just a week after the Court issued *Franchise Tax Board*, Justice Sotomayor and the four other liberal Justices, joined by Justice Neil Gorsuch, voted in *Herrera v. Wyoming* to overturn an over one-hundred-year-old precedent and uphold the validity of a Crow Indian treaty from 1868. The Justice's debates over whether and when to overturn precedent have at times been confusing and amusing, as both conservatives and liberals have postured themselves as the defenders of precedent, and by extension, of the Rule of Law and even the Supreme Court itself. But throughout these debates, *Roe's* vulnerability has been the subtext of the conflict.

Webster v. Reproductive Health Services in 1989 bruited this debate in the context of a Missouri abortion control statute. Justice Anthony Kennedy wrote to Chief Justice William Rehnquist shortly before the Court's decision regarding Rehnquist's draft opinion for the Court, and cc'd the Justices who would make up the *Webster* majority—Byron White, Sandra Day O'Connor and Antonin Scalia. Kennedy told Rehnquist:

> *I am in substantial agreement with your excellent opinion in this case. As you know, in my view the case does provide a fair opportunity to assess the continuing validity of* Roe v. Wade, *and I would have used the occasion to overrule that case and*

return this difficult issue to the political systems of the states. But overruling Roe *is not a strict necessity here, so I anticipate being able to join an opinion for the Court as you have circulated it …*

The Court's plurality, with Chief Justice Rehnquist writing, upheld provisions of Missouri's abortion statute, but expressly refused to overturn *Roe*, in a part of the decision in which Justices White and Kennedy joined. "This case therefore affords us no occasion to revisit the holding of *Roe* … and we leave it undisturbed," the Court's plurality said.

Justice Scalia was disappointed and direct, saying he would have overturned *Roe*, and charging the court with "contriv[ing] to avoid doing it." Scalia demonstrated a thoughtful understanding of the question politics should (and should not) play in the Court, arguing that avoiding a constitutional question because of concerns external to the case like public response is, itself, "political" and injurious to the Court's integrity and reputation:

> *The outcome of today's case will doubtless be heralded as a triumph of judicial self-awarded sovereignty over a field where it has little proper business since the answers to most of the cruel questions posed are political and not juridical—a sovereignty which therefore quite properly, but to the great damage of the Court, makes it the object of the sort of organized public pressure that political institutions in a democracy ought to receive.*
>
> *Our retaining control, through* Roe, *of what I believe to be, and many of our citizens recognize to be, a political issue, continuously distorts the public perception of the role of this Court. We can now look forward to at least another Term with carts full of mail from the public, and streets full of demonstrators, urging us— their unelected and life tenured judges who have been awarded those extraordinary, undemocratic characteristics precisely in order that we might follow the law despite the popular will—to follow the popular will.*

Three years later, another plurality in *Planned Parenthood v. Casey* voted to affirm *Roe v. Wade*, including Justice Anthony Kennedy, who changed his mind about overturning *Roe* shortly before the decision was issued and provided the deciding vote. The plurality relied on considerations external to the constitutional text, and explicitly the public's perceived embrace of the right to abortion in the years since *Roe*. "For two decades of economic and social developments, people have organized intimate relationships and made choices that define their views of themselves and their places in society in reliance on the availability of abortion, in the event that contraception should fail," the plurality reasoned. Once again, the plurality cited the fierce political debate over abortion as a reason to maintain the rule of *Roe*, in the hope that by doing so, that debate would subside. "Whether or not a new social consensus is developing on [abortion], its divisiveness is no less today than in 1973, and pressure to overrule the decision, like pressure to retain it, has grown only more intense. A decision to overrule *Roe*'s essential holding under the existing circumstances would address error, if error there was, at the cost of both profound and unnecessary damage to the Court's legitimacy, and to the Nation's commitment to the rule of law. It is therefore imperative to adhere to the essence of *Roe*'s original decision, and we do so today." So for the *Casey* plurality, adherence to the Rule of Law mandated acquiescing to public demand for abortion—a perverse distortion of the meaning of the principle.

The only safe channel between the Scylla of public opposition to a Supreme Court decision and the Charybdis of public support for it is to hew only to the principle of federal judicial review on which the Constitution and the federal judiciary is founded. The only way for the Court to avoid looking political is not to be political; the text and history of the Constitution should be the only basis for the Court's interpretation of the nation's charter. Or as Chief Justice John Marshall put it in another case, *Marbury v. Madison*, it is the Court's duty finally—and merely—to "say what the law is."

9

One New Justice Can Impact Laws Regarding Gun Regulation

Nina Totenberg

Nina Totenberg is legal affairs correspondent for National Public Radio. She reports regularly on the NPR programs All Things Considered, Morning Edition, *and* Weekend Edition. *Her work often focuses on the activities of the Supreme Court.*

Gun regulation is one of the most intense and acrimonious issues in American politics. Because the entire issue is framed by the Second Amendment right to bear arms, specific controversies are generally subject to constitutional interpretation and thus fall within the purview of the Supreme Court. In this viewpoint, the author examines the recent gun rights case New York State Rifle and Pistol Association Inc. vs. City of New York *and suggests that new justices Neil Gorsuch and Brett Kavanaugh may sway the balance of the court in favor of private gun rights. (The court dismissed this case as moot in 2020 after New York City amended the rule the case hinged on.)*

G uns: when and how to regulate them. It's one of the biggest issues across the country. But the US Supreme Court has rarely weighed in on the issue. In modern times, it has ruled decisively just twice. Now it's on the brink of doing so again.

With the retirement of Justice Anthony Kennedy, there now are five conservative justices who may be willing to shut down many attempts at regulation, just as the NRA's lock on state legislatures may be waning.

For the past decade, the court has been wary of gun cases. In 2008 the court ruled for the first time that the Second Amendment right to bear arms is an individual right. Two years later, the court said that right applied to state laws, not just federal laws regulating gun ownership and use. Since then, however, there has been radio silence as the justices have turned away challenges, one after another, to gun laws across the country. Until now.

On Monday the court hears arguments in a case from New York, a city and a state with some of the toughest gun regulations in the country. Several gun owners and the NRA's New York affiliate challenged the rules for having a handgun at home. They contended the city gun license was so restrictive it was unconstitutional.

Specifically, they said the state law and city regulations violated the right to bear arms because they forbid handgun owners from carrying their pistols anywhere other than seven firing ranges within the city limits. That meant that pistol owners could not carry their guns to a second home, or to shooting ranges or competitions in other states nearby. The lower courts upheld the regulations as justified to protect safety in the most densely populated city in the country.

But when the Supreme Court agreed to hear the gun owners' appeal, the state and the city changed the law to allow handgun owners to transport their locked and unloaded guns to second homes or shooting ranges outside the city.

"Won't Say 'Yes' for an Answer"

With those changes, the first question Monday will be whether the case is moot and should be thrown out because New York has already given the gun owners everything they asked for in their lawsuit.

"This is an instance where it appears the petitioners won't say 'yes' for an answer," says James Johnson, counsel for the city of New York.

But former Solicitor General Paul Clement, who represents the gun owners, counters that the amended regulations still give the city too much power to regulate.

"The city of New York never expressed any doubt about the constitutionality of these regulations when they were winning in the district court and the court of appeals," argues Clement. "And then lo and behold, all of a sudden the city decides you know maybe we don't need these regulations after all."

And, he observes, the city is still defending the original regulations.

The city is indeed doing that because the justices refused in October to throw the case out on mootness grounds, opting instead to hear the mootness arguments today, along with the direct challenge to the regulations themselves.

Defending Nonexistent Laws

That does put the city in a weird position. The city is forced to defend regulations that are no longer in place, and that it claims it has no intention of reviving.

"It's our position that by justifiably restricting the ability to carry firearms broadly on the streets of New York, it contributes to making the city safe," says Johnson.

And there's the rub. What did the Supreme Court mean in its 2008 decision when it said that the right to bear arms is an individual right? Back then, Justice Antonin Scalia, writing for the five justice court majority, framed the right most explicitly as the right to own a gun for self-defense in one's home.

Moreover, the opinion contained a paragraph of specific qualifiers that, according to court sources, were added to Scalia's opinion at the insistence of Justice Kennedy, who provided the fifth vote needed to prevail in the case. The court said, for instance, that its opinion "cast no doubt on" longstanding bans on "carrying firearms in sensitive places such as schools and government buildings, or bans on dangerous and unusual weapons."

"It Will Make a Difference That Justice Kavanaugh Is on the Court."

But Kennedy—who insisted on that limiting language—has now retired, replaced by Justice Brett Kavanaugh. And Kavanaugh, as a lower court judge, wrote in favor of expansive gun rights.

"I do think it will make a difference that Justice Kavanaugh is on the court," says the gun owners' Clement.

He notes that not only does Kavanaugh have a record sympathetic to broad gun rights, but that the new justice was constrained by the court's precedents when he sat on the lower court.

"Now he can interpret the Constitution in a different way in his new perch," says Clement. "He's somebody who I would think is going to be receptive to arguments that the Second Amendment fully protects an individual right and is not strictly limited to the home."

Manhattan: 1.6 Million Residents in 23 Square Miles

New York argues that the history of gun ownership dating back to Colonial times shows that in this densely populated city, the law forbids the discharge of firearms on "any street, lane, alley, garden or other places where people frequently walk." And by 1784 the state regulated the storage and transport of gun powder, too.

Today, as the city observes in its briefs, the city is far and away the most densely populated city in the country, with 27,000 residents per square mile. Manhattan alone packs around 1.6 million residents into 23 square miles, and that population doubles every weekday with commuters. These people, plus tens of thousands of tourists, move through the city's crowded streets, traveling "to, near and around a staggering concentration of sensitive places such as schools, daycare centers, government buildings, playgrounds and places of worship"—all places that the Supreme Court seemed to say in 2008 are legitimate places to ban guns.

Countering that argument, lawyer Clement maintains that the Founding Fathers never intended the right to own a gun to be limited to the home. At the very minimum, he notes, our Founders allowed gun owners to carry their firearms from one place to another.

Libraries Are Not Lethal

Like any good advocate, Clement is offering the justices alternative routes to a gun-friendly ruling.

"They could say the Second Amendment is not limited strictly to the home and therefore this regulation has to go," says Clement. Even that, he would see as a major victory.

The alternative and broader ruling, he says, would treat the right to own a gun in the same way that limits on free speech are treated. With considerable suspicion.

"I don't think anybody would think that if the city of New York said, you know we have seven perfectly nice libraries in the city of New York and there's really no reason for any of you to go to libraries in New Jersey," posits Clement. "Everybody would recognize that that's clearly a First Amendment problem."

Johnson, the city's lawyer, dismisses that analogy, noting that libraries have no "lethality."

"It Kind of Falls on Me"

And that's something at least one of the individual plaintiffs on the gun-rights side thinks. Retired NYC bus driver Efrain Alvarez is one of the three individuals joining the New York State Rifle & Pistol Association to challenge this law.

"If a bad apple grabs a gun and he does something stupid, it kind of falls on me because I'm part of what's going on," Alvarez said in an interview with Reuters. In that same interview, he said he admires the NRA but sometimes disagrees with its policies.

Alvarez has had his handgun license suspended twice in the past decade. Most recently the city confiscated 45 firearms, including five handguns, from a steel vault in his back bedroom. But he likely will get them back, as he says he has accepted a plea deal from the Bronx district attorney that would drop the most recent charge against him if he is not arrested for six months.

None of this is actually related to the current Supreme Court case. The 64-year-old bus driver is a gun enthusiast and hunter who told Reuters that he joined the lawsuit because he thought it was ridiculous that he could own a handgun but not be able to travel with it to compete.

Lawyers for Alvarez and the lawyers on the other side know that if the Supreme Court rules on the merits of the now-defunct regulations, it will be a very big deal for one simple reason: It will be only the third decision on gun rights in modern times, and it will inevitably lay down some new guidelines for lower courts to follow when gun regulations are challenged.

10

The Purview of the US Supreme Court Is Evolving

Eric Black

Eric Black is a US-based journalist and columnist for the online publication MinnPost. *Previously he was a reporter for the* Minnesota Star Tribune.

The United States Constitution grants specific authorities to the Supreme Court. Such authorities are subject to interpretation in various ways. The impact of the court and its decisions depends a great deal on how the court understands and exercises its own authority, and that understanding has evolved through the course of US history. Using examples like the Roe v. Wade *and* Citizen's United *decisions, this viewpoint suggests that the court has become more involved in the policymaking process in ways that were perhaps never intended by the framers of the Constitution.*

S o the authority of the US Supreme Court to strike down laws is not explicitly enumerated in the Constitution, was established by the court itself in a case filled with conflicts of interest for the court itself, and its absolute nature was questioned by the likes of Thomas Jefferson, Andrew Jackson and Abraham Lincoln. So what? I'm not under any illusion that it is going away and am not arguing that our system would be better without it, although there are times when I have my doubts.

"How the Supreme Court Has Come to Play a Policymaking Role," by Eric Black, *MinnPost*, November 20, 2012. Reprinted by permission.

Officially, US Supreme Court justices (and especially nominees to the court during their confirmation hearings) subscribe to a doctrine of "judicial modesty," which suggests that—in a democracy—the least democratic branch should overrule the policy preferences of the more democratic branches only when the conflict between a law and the Constitution is strong and clear and never when the justices simply have a different policy preference from the legislators.

Trouble is, no one can define or enforce those limits other than the justices themselves. When they impose their policy preferences in the guise of defending the Constitution—or even when they are perceived to be doing so—the credibility of the whole system takes a hit.

In reality, compared to Supreme Courts in other democracies around the world, ours is more powerful than most, perhaps more than any. There are several reasons for this. University of Chicago Law Professor Tom Ginsburg, who directs a project comparing every Constitution adopted since 1787, notes a couple of the big reasons. In an interview, Ginsburg said that the US Constitution is way below average in length, covers many fewer topics than typical more recent constitution do, and therefore leaves more scope for Supreme Court justices to fill in the blanks on the many new areas that have arisen since 1787. Our Constitution is "venerated as sacred," Ginsburg said, which is a barrier to any proposal to change it, and, in addition, the requirements for amending it are more onerous.

"My argument is that all of these factors perversely empower the Supreme Court and makes the court much more likely to engage in public policy" than high courts of other nations, Ginsburg said.

Two landmark decisions that are part of our everyday politics illustrate the lack of real judicial modesty and demonstrate how the court has come to play a policymaking role that is supposed to be reserved for elected officials. The cases are *Roe v. Wade* and *Citizens United v. Federal Election Commission*.

Roe v. Wade

In *Roe*, the court discovered a constitutional right to abortion (even though the word "abortion" certainly doesn't appear in the Constitution). The majority found this right to be a part of a general right to privacy guaranteed by the Constitution (even though the word "privacy" also appears nowhere in the Constitution). There are some rights guaranteed by the Constitution that have something to do with privacy, like the Fourth Amendment right to be free in your home from warrantless searches by the authorities. And the court had previously discovered other unenumerated privacy- (and contraception-) related rights that a majority of justices ruled were guaranteed by the Constitution.

I recognize that most liberals and many people reading this article revere the *Roe* decision, which is also part of the point.

Before *Roe*, the abortion question was left to the states. Some allowed the procedure, most banned it. To think that women should have a right to choose for themselves whether to have an abortion is an utterly defensible belief and one I share. To think that the authors and/or ratifiers of the Bill of Rights had abortion in mind when they described the basic rights that must be beyond encroachment by the government would be ludicrous. In fact, no one seriously asserts that.

If such a policy is to become the law of the land, or of individual states, it would certainly be best if it came from the elected branches, which are assigned the task of making laws and policies.

In *Roe*, the majority not only amended the Bill of Rights to insert a new right that the original authors hadn't intended, but went further into what one might call a legislative mode by breaking a pregnancy into trimesters and specifying different levels of a woman's discretion over the abortion choice during each trimester.

To strict constructionists, and especially to abortion opponents, *Roe* became and has remained the leading symbol of "legislating from the bench." It was a statement from the court's majority that they needed little basis in the Constitution to create rights that they felt should be guaranteed. In an earlier 1958 ruling, the court declared that the meaning of language in the Constitution was not frozen in time according to what it meant when it was written but "must draw its meaning from the evolving standards of decency that mark the progress of a maturing society."

The *Roe* ruling has been central to public perceptions of the Supreme Court ever since. For example, *Roe* remains the sub rosa litmus test around all appointments to the court, which is the subject of the next installment of this series. For purposes of this installment, suffice it to say that in *Roe*, the court appointed itself the key body in charge of legislating and regulating in the area of abortion.

And two years ago, the court did the same in the area of campaign finance.

Citizens United v. Federal Election Commission

Not long after the *Roe* decision (January 1973), the Watergate scandal culminated in the resignation of President Richard Nixon. The scandal, among other things, alerted the country to the cesspool of secret money and contributions-for-influence that had engulfed the Nixon reelection campaign of 1972.

In two waves, Congress responded to shelter the system from the threat of influence-buying-via-campaign-finance: In 1974, with a set of amendments to the Federal Elections Commission Act; in 2002, with the Bipartisan Campaign Reform Act (usually known as McCain-Feingold after the senators who sponsored it).

Taken together, the laws set out key principles that Congress believed would strike an appropriate (and constitutional) balance between the importance of free speech in an election context, and the need to reduce the corrupting influence of big money over politics. The principles included:

- Allowing individuals to give unlimited contributions was an invitation to corruption, so each individual should be limited to a $1,000 contribution to a candidate per campaign cycle.
- Contributions should be disclosed promptly.

- Candidates should be required to take responsibility for the ads run on their behalf by including a message, in the candidate's own voice, that he or she "approved this message."
- Neither corporations nor labor unions should be allowed to spend funds directly from their treasuries on electioneering messages (basically ads that mention a candidate by name).
- For presidential elections, a voluntary system of public finance should be created. A candidate who agreed to limit the amount of money he accepted from private parties would be eligible for federal matching funds so that theoretically, a candidate who didn't sell out to the highest bidder might still be able to run a competitive race.

In two rulings (*Buckley v. Valeo* in 1974 and *Citizens United* in 2010), the Supreme Court struck down portions of both acts, and either eliminated or undermined the effect of each of those five features on the grounds that they violated the First Amendment guarantee of freedom of speech.

What we now have is a ridiculous system that is more loophole than law. But the main point for our purposes is that the ridiculous system is the creation of the Supreme Court, which used the power of judicial review to expropriate from Congress the role of lawmaker in the area of campaign finance. Like the system of abortion regulation since *Roe*, the system of campaign finance we have is the Supreme Court's system.

Money = Speech

The court ruled in *Buckley* that an individual can spend an unlimited amount of his own money to promote himself for election. Allowing a candidate to say whatever he might choose to say is not enough freedom of speech, the court ruled, if he or she cannot spend an unlimited amount to broadcast his message. The political parties soon recognized the advantage of nominating very wealthy candidates who can "self-fund" their campaigns, because that frees their other donors up to contribute money to other races. As a result, the Senate is now more of a Millionaires Club than ever. Is that good for democracy? The court doesn't say, only that the First Amendment requires it.

Corporate Personhood

The court ruled in *Citizens United*—again on First Amendment grounds—that corporations and unions can spend directly from their treasuries to influence elections. Previous Supreme Courts had ruled that a corporation is a kind of person and has some (not necessarily all) of the constitutional rights of "natural persons," namely individual US citizens. *Citizens United* simply applied this principle to the right of corporations to express themselves politically. Is this good for democracy? Does it help reduce the potential corruption of politics by money? Seems unlikely. The court doesn't say.

Citizens United actually implied that disclosure requirements were constitutional, so long as they didn't create too much of a burden on the donor corporations to comply. This issue is still in play in multiple cases working their way through the appellate courts. Many donors, especially the corporate ones, don't want their contributions disclosed because they might get blowback from customers who don't like the corporation's politics. The organizations receiving the contributions have been challenging the disclosure requirements as unduly burdensome. The most recent appellate rulings have favored non-disclosure. At the moment, the idea that full, prompt, clear disclosure of the sources of political contributions is an important part of the campaign finance scheme is in full retreat.

Of course, the organizations that we call SuperPACs have arisen to exploit the many loopholes that the court left open. Because of the way SuperPACs are organized, individuals (including those who are not themselves candidates) and corporations (giving directly from their treasuries and without needing the approval of their shareholders) can give unlimited amounts to SuperPACs.

Unlimited. This is how we get a figure like casino magnate Sheldon Adelson (net worth: $20 billion; ranking on *Forbes* list of richest Americans: seventh), who gave $10 million to try to make

Newt Gingrich the Republican nominee and who was reported ready and willing to spend $100 million to make Mitt Romney president. This is very good for owners of TV stations in swing states who sell advertising during campaign season. Is it good for democracy? Congress thought it wasn't and tried to make this level of individual giving impossible. The Supreme Court made it possible on free speech grounds. When Adelson gives those millions to organizations that run ads that he hasn't written, hasn't even reviewed, is he really speaking?

SuperPACs have now become so active that they spend more money on political advertising than the candidates' own campaign committees do. As a result, although a candidate still must take responsibility ("I approve this message") for the ads run by his own campaign committee, more and more of the ads are run by SuperPACs and other groups that are technically not associated with the candidates they support. The SuperPACs go by generic names that tell you nothing about who is behind the ad, names like "American Crossroads" or "American Bridge" or "PrioritiesUSA" or "Restore Our future" or "Winning Our Future" or "Make Us Great Again" or "Red, White and Blue." SuperPAC ads generally carry the Orwellian disclaimer: "Not authorized by any candidate or candidate's committee."

An informal system seems to have emerged in which the candidates run the nicer ads and the SuperPACs run the nastier ones with the heavier doses of half-truths. When the candidate is asked about the nasty ads and the half truths, he can (and often does) say that he hasn't even seen the ad in question, and takes no responsibility for it. The legal requirement that candidates stand by their ads has been substantially defeated. Is this good for democracy?

In that I-take-no-responsibility-for-it moment, the candidate will also often mention that he is in fact prohibited by law from having anything to do with the ads run by SuperPACs that support him nor anything to do with the SuperPAC itself.

Independent and Uncoordinated

That's true. Justice Anthony Kennedy, who wrote the majority opinion in *Citizens United*, recognized that unlimited donations could lead to the kind of corruption associated with Watergate. So he insisted in his ruling that organizations that are not working directly for candidates must be "independent" and cannot "coordinate" their activities with the candidates' committees.

The idea that SuperPACs are independent of and uncoordinated with the candidates—except in the most meaningless technical sense necessary to comply with Justice Kennedy's requirement—is laughable. PrioritiesUSA, the leading pro-Obama SuperPAC in the election cycle that just ended, was founded and run by two former officials of the Obama White House. One of them, Bill Burton, was the chief spokesman for the 2008 Obama campaign and then Obama's deputy press secretary for most of his term before leaving to start PrioritiesUSA. He hardly needed daily telephone contact with the 2012 Obama reelection campaign to tailor PrioritiesUSA's advertising strategy to fit the needs of the overall Obama reelection effort.

The most active pro-Romney SuperPAC was Restore Our Future. Its board of directors included Charles Spies, who served as general counsel of Romney's 2008 presidential campaign; Carl Forti, who was political director of Romney's 2008 campaign; and Larry McCarthy, a media adviser to Romney in '08. Restore Our Future got the largest portion of its funds from Wall Street interests. One group of Romney supporters, to ensure their anonymity, actually created a dummy LLC (limited liability corporation) in March of 2011, donated $1 million via the corporation to Restore Our Future in April, then dissolved the corporation in July.

The last of the five measures I laid out above that Congress enacted to try to control donors' power over politics was public matching funds. Technically, presidential candidates still have the ability to get public funds for their campaigns, if they are willing to abide by limits on how much they will raise by other means. But in the post-*Citizens United* age, it may never again be practical for a campaign to accept the limits, knowing that their opponent's campaign can raise unimaginable amounts. This year, for the first time, both presidential campaigns rejected the public funds in order to avoid the limits that come with them.

So, to Review

The Constitution gave us the First Amendment, which guarantees freedom of expression. It put Congress in charge of making laws, the president in charge of enforcing them and the Supreme Court in charge of deciding cases that arise under them, including cases in which the laws may conflict with the constitutional guarantees.

Freedom of expression is not absolute. Fire-in-a-crowded-theater and all that. Personally, I don't believe that a society in which there are reasonable limits on the amount an individual or a corporation can give to carpet bomb the airwaves with 30-second attack ads in the last weeks of an election campaign would necessarily be a society without freedom of expression. The Supreme Court has, in fact, ruled that Congress is constitutionally empowered to take steps to protect the political process from corruption, including corruption by money. Nonetheless, the Supreme Court has vitiated every measure the Congress has adopted to promote that objective.

The court divided 5-4 on the *Citizens United* case.

In a long dissent, Justice John Paul Stevens wrote:

A democracy cannot function effectively when its constituent members believe laws are being bought and sold... At bottom, the Court's opinion is thus a rejection of the common sense of the American people, who have recognized a need to prevent corporations from undermining self government since the founding, and who have fought against the distinctive corrupting potential of corporate electioneering since the days of Theodore Roosevelt. It is a strange time to repudiate that common sense. While American democracy is imperfect, few outside the majority of this Court would have thought its flaws included a dearth of corporate money in politics.

11

Republicans Set a Dangerous Precedent in Ignoring the Nomination of Merrick Garland

Ron Elving

Ron Elving is senior editor for NPR News and a member of the faculty at American University. He was previously political editor for USA Today and for Congressional Quarterly.

This piece looks at the case of US circuit court judge Merrick Garland, who was nominated to the Supreme Court in 2016 by then president Barack Obama. Congressional Republicans refused to even meet with Garland or hold hearings on his nomination, arguing that it was an election year and that the next president should make the nomination (a position they would abandon four years later when they rushed Amy Coney Barrett through the confirmation process just before the 2020 presidential election). For many observers, congressional Republicans' position represented a stark and dangerous departure from constitutional precedent, and one that was almost certain to further politicize the Supreme Court.

So much has happened in the past two years that many may have forgotten what happened to Merrick Garland in the spring of 2016.

But filling in that recollection goes some distance in explaining a lot of what has happened since.

To recap, Garland was nominated to fill the 2016 vacancy on the Supreme Court created by the death that February of Justice Antonin Scalia, an icon of conservative jurisprudence.

President Barack Obama quickly named Merrick Garland, then 63, to fill the seat. Garland had long been considered a prime prospect for the high court, serving as chief judge on the US Court of Appeals for the District of Columbia Circuit—a frequent source of justices that is sometimes called the "little Supreme Court."

Widely regarded as a moderate, Garland had been praised in the past by many Republicans, including influential senators such as Orrin Hatch of Utah.

But even before Obama had named Garland, and in fact only hours after Scalia's death was announced, Senate Majority Leader Mitch McConnell declared any appointment by the sitting president to be null and void. He said the next Supreme Court justice should be chosen by the next president—to be elected later that year.

"Of course," said McConnell, "the American people should have a say in the court's direction. It is a president's constitutional right to nominate a Supreme Court justice, and it is the Senate's constitutional right to act as a check on the president and withhold its consent."

Supreme Court picks have often been controversial. There have been contentious hearings and floor debates and contested votes. But to ignore the nominee entirely, as if no vacancy existed?

There was no precedent for such an action since the period around the Civil War and Reconstruction. No Democratic president had made an appointment while Republicans held the Senate since 1895.

In a speech that August in Kentucky, McConnell would say: "One of my proudest moments was when I looked Barack Obama in the eye and I said, 'Mr. President, you will not fill the Supreme Court vacancy.'"

McConnell was not alone. The 11 Republican members of the Senate Judiciary Committee signed a letter saying they had no intention of consenting to any nominee from Obama. No proceedings of any kind were held on Garland's appointment.

The court had to convene that October with only eight justices, divided often between the four appointed by Democrats and the four appointed by Republicans. Short-handed, the court deadlocked on a number of issues and declined to hear others.

Democrats were outraged, of course, but were short of tools with which to respond. As the minority party—following a disastrous midterm in 2014—they could not force a committee or a floor vote. They gave speeches, and they urged voters to turn out in protest in the November elections.

Scores of scholars—law professors, historians and political scientists—urged the Senate to at least have a process for Garland as a duly appointed nominee with impeccable qualifications. But some lawyers and academics pointed out that the Constitution empowered the Senate to "advise and consent" but did not require it do so. (Some adding that they thought the Senate still ought to do so.)

A federal lawsuit was filed to compel McConnell to hold a vote on Garland. It was thrown out because a judge said the plaintiff, as an ordinary voter, had no standing to sue.

For his part, McConnell argued that the Democrats had at least contemplated a similar tactic back in 1992, when Obama's vice president, Joe Biden, was chairman of the Senate Judiciary Committee and mused about urging President George H.W. Bush to withhold any nominees to the high court until the end of the "political season."

At the time, the Senate had just been through a bruising battle over the 1991 confirmation of Justice Clarence Thomas.

As it happened, no vacancy occurred in 1992. But McConnell and others referred to the "Biden rule" nonetheless in justifying the blockade of Garland.

With or without such justification, McConnell's blockade was doubly effective just as a power move.

First, it prevented the seating of a Democratic president's choice. Had he been considered, Garland might have pulled a few majority-party members across the aisle. Supreme Court nominees nearly always win at least some votes from the party opposing the president, and Garland had a strong law-and-order history. Had he performed well on TV, voting against him might have been harder—especially for Republicans seeking re-election in competitive states.

Second, and more important, the vacancy became a powerful motivator for conservative voters in the fall. Many saw a vote for Trump as a means to keep Scalia's seat away from the liberals and give the appointment to someone who promised to name anti-abortion justices supportive of Second Amendment gun rights.

Again and again in the fall, candidate Donald Trump treated the Supreme Court as a touchstone, sometimes simply shouting the two words to his rally crowds. And indeed, polling has shown the court vacancy did mean a great deal to Trump voters, especially those religious conservatives who had personal misgivings about him.

Now, of course, McConnell's calculus has changed. With a slim but steady majority of the Senate, and Vice President Mike Pence available to break a tie, McConnell feels confident he can confirm Trump's nominee and get his people out to vote again—this time, in gratitude.

Democrats see all this as what their Senate leader Chuck Schumer called "the height of hypocrisy." But will that move voters in their direction more now than it did in 2016 or motivate the disaffected within their base?

Some say the Democrats hurt themselves two years ago, first with a nominee who would not excite the party's base. Whatever his evident virtues, Garland was another white male who, as a 63-year-old moderate, could not promise decades as a liberal warrior.

There is also ample evidence that the Supreme Court motivates conservatives more than it does progressives. That has often been the case since the *Roe v. Wade* abortion legalization decision in

1973 launched an era of social issue backlash that split the old Democratic coalition.

It also has been argued that the Democrats caved to McConnell's pressure tactics in the Garland case. They should have found a way to force a vote or "shut down the Senate" to light a spark.

But Democrats are generally averse to government shutdown strategies, especially considering the potential blowback on their own candidates. In 2016, it was still the Obama era and the Democrats' executive administration. Shutdowns rarely help the party perceived to be in power, even if it's not really in control.

So it was safer, in the judgments of spring and summer 2016, to let the Republicans look intransigent and unfair and hope somebody noticed. Perhaps the injustice to Garland would help Democrats win seats in supposedly blue states such as Wisconsin and Pennsylvania, and even red ones such as Missouri and North Carolina.

Instead, the country moved on. There were highly contentious primaries in both parties and plenty of other news to preoccupy everyone.

Besides, and lest we forget, the Senate Democrats and most everyone else thought they had an insurance policy on the Scalia vacancy. The assumption was that Hillary Clinton would be elected. Clinton, who did, after all, win the popular vote by several million votes, might even have helped carry in a Democratic Senate. And then she could have renominated Garland, or someone younger and more liberal.

As it sorted out, the Democrats were cautious, overconfident and misinformed about the mood of the country. They lost in Wisconsin, Pennsylvania, Missouri and North Carolina, winding up still in the minority.

That left them powerless to stop McConnell from eliminating the filibuster for Supreme Court nominees in 2017, paving the way to confirmation of Trump's first choice and probably his second.

And that is the predicament in which they find themselves today.

12

Confirming Brett Kavanaugh Became a Battle

Tom McCarthy

Tom McCarthy is an American journalist currently serving as national affairs correspondent for Guardian US.

This viewpoint, published in the final days of the battle to confirm Supreme Court Justice Brett Kavanaugh, provides an overview of the controversy that erupted around Kavanaugh's nomination when he was publicly accused of sexual assault by multiple women. The acrimonious Kavanaugh hearings, like those that followed the nominations of Robert Bork and Clarence Thomas years before, contributed to a widespread perception that Supreme Court nominations have been all but subsumed by partisan warfare. Kavanaugh's nomination was even more complicated because of Democrats' simmering anger over congressional Republicans' previous refusal to consider President Obama's nomination of Merrick Garland. On every level, the Kavanaugh affair reflected the tawdry and aggressive politics that increasingly characterize Supreme Court nominations in America.

The US Senate is preparing for a final vote on the nomination of Judge Brett Kavanaugh to the Supreme Court. Here's where things stand in the controversial battle that has roiled American politics for weeks.

"Q&A: Brett Kavanaugh's Controversial Confirmation Battle Explained," by Tom McCarthy, Guardian News & Media Limited, October 5, 2018. Reprinted by permission.

When Will the Senate Vote?

On Friday morning the Senate voted 51-49 to end debate on the nomination, setting up a final vote on Kavanaugh to be held over the weekend, likely on Saturday. In Friday's vote, known as a cloture vote, two senators voted against their parties: Republican senator Lisa Murkowski voted no, and Democratic senator Joe Manchin voted yes.

For Kavanaugh to be defeated, two senators who voted to end debate on his nomination, effectively allowing it to proceed, would ultimately have to vote against him. If the senators split 50-50, Vice-President Mike Pence would break the tie in Kavanaugh's favor, in what would be an unprecedented move to install a Supreme Court justice.

What Happened in the Last Week?

The FBI interviewed a reported nine people about at least two separate incidents of sexual assault allegedly perpetrated by Kavanaugh, allegations he denies.

Democrats called the investigation a sham. Republicans said it was thorough.

The investigation was opened after Dr Christine Blasey Ford, a California professor, testified last week that she had been sexually assaulted at a house party by Kavanaugh when she was 15 years old and he was 17. She said Kavanaugh's friend Mark Judge was in the room cheering the future judge on. Kavanaugh vehemently denied the account.

The FBI interviewed Judge. They also interviewed the second woman to accuse Kavanaugh of assault, Deborah Ramirez, a former classmate of Kavanaugh's at Yale who said he exposed himself to her at a dorm party. Kavanaugh also denied that accusation.

Senators spent Thursday reviewing a closely held FBI report on its findings. The judiciary committee chairman, Chuck Grassley, said the report contained "nothing that we didn't already know." The White House thought the report vindicated Kavanaugh, the *Wall Street Journal* reported.

The limited FBI investigation was proposed by the Republican senator Jeff Flake last week as a way to ensure the Senate handled Ford's allegations—and protesters' concerns—responsibly. Democrats called for a thorough investigation.

Was the Investigation Thorough?

Democrats and some Republican figures—though no Republican senators—are saying that the investigation was not at all thorough. They say the FBI failed to speak with dozens of potential witnesses. Here's a breakdown:

The Ford Incident

Ford herself was not interviewed. Nor was Kavanaugh. In a letter to the FBI, lawyers for Ford said: "We are profoundly disappointed that after the tremendous sacrifice she made in coming forward, those directing the FBI investigation were not interested in seeking the truth."

They submitted a list of at least 22 people willing to speak with the FBI who might have been able to provide relevant testimony. None were contacted.

The Ramirez Incident

Lawyers for Ramirez sent the FBI a list of more than 20 people who might be able to corroborate her story. None appear to have been contacted. One former suitemate of Kavanaugh, Kenneth G Appold, told the *New Yorker* that he remembered hearing about the incident at the time. He was not interviewed.

Possible False Statements

Multiple people have stepped forward in the past week to say that Kavanaugh misled the Senate about his youthful drinking and other details. In a piece for Slate, former Kavanaugh roommate James Roche said Kavanaugh "stood up under oath and lied about his drinking and about the meaning of words in his yearbook," which Roche said referred to sexual activity despite Kavanaugh's denials.

On Thursday, the New Jersey senator Robert Menendez called the FBI inquiry "a bullsh*t investigation."

What Else Has Happened?

Donald Trump mocked Ford, who admitted to not remembering certain details of the alleged assault, at a campaign-style rally on Tuesday with a question-and-answer patter that brought cheers from a crowd in Southaven, Mississippi.

"How did you get home?" Trump said, echoing a question Ford was asked by the committee. "I don't remember," the president said.

"How did you get there? 'I don't remember.' Where is the place? 'I don't remember.' How many years ago was it? 'I don't know.' What neighborhood was it? 'I don't know.' Where's the house? 'I don't know.'"

Trump concluded the riff by lamenting the personal cost to Kavanaugh of Ford's allegations and by insinuating that Ford was part of a partisan conspiracy. "They destroy people; these are really evil people," Trump said.

Last Saturday, meanwhile, Matt Damon sent up Kavanaugh on *Saturday Night Live*.

Late on Thursday, Kavanaugh took the unusual move of publishing an op-ed in the *Wall Street Journal* titled "I am an independent, impartial judge." The piece sought to address concerns about his demeanor after he repeatedly lashed out in Senate testimony and blamed the pressure on him over his alleged past violent conduct on the Clintons.

"I was very emotional last Thursday, more so than I have ever been," Kavanaugh wrote. "I might have been too emotional at times. I know that my tone was sharp, and I said a few things I should not have said."

Does It Look Like He'll Be Confirmed?

It's close. If the final vote reflects Friday's cloture vote (to end the debate), Kavanaugh will be confirmed. If only one senator who voted to end debate switches sides to oppose Kavanaugh, he will be confirmed. But the situation remains fluid and hard to predict.

Is Justice Kavanaugh a Fait Accompli?

The activists on Capitol Hill don't think so.

13

Talk of Expanding the Supreme Court Has a Long History

Mark Walsh

Mark Walsh is a journalist whose work focuses on the US Supreme Court. His writing has appeared in the American Bar Association Journal, *in* Education Week, *on* C-SPAN, *and on* National Public Radio.

This viewpoint examines the history of proposals to alter the structure and/or expand the size of the United States Supreme Court. The size of the court changed several times early in the country's history, but it has stood as a nine-member body since the nineteenth century. Since then, numerous proposals—some more serious than others— have emerged to expand the size of the court. The author focuses particularly on President Franklin Delano Roosevelt's failed "court-packing" plan in 1936 and compares the controversy over that effort to more recent debates.

T he US Constitution's Article III says the judicial power of the nation "shall be vested in one supreme court." It says nothing about how many justices should serve on the court.

That has led to a range of sizes throughout US history—from five to 10 authorized seats on the court. Now, those advocating an expansion of the high court by two, four, six or some other number of seats are having their moment.

"Justice by Numbers: Proposals Resurface to Expand the Size of the Court," by Mark Walsh, American Bar Association, May 1, 2019. Reprinted by permission.

In recent months, a concept that has been on the fringes of political theory has suddenly gained steam, with several progressive organizations calling for an expansion of the court and pushing Democratic presidential candidates to respond to the idea.

The idea is that if the Democrats win the White House and Senate in next year's election and retain control of the House of Representatives, they could push for the additional seats on the high court. And those seats would presumably be filled with new left-leaning justices who would shift the balance away from the court's conservative majority.

"We are in a dire democracy emergency in which the Supreme Court has belonged to the Republican Party and the donor class," says Aaron Belkin, a political science professor at San Francisco State University and the executive director of Pack the Courts, a fledgling organization that calls for adding four seats.

"A Hostile Supreme Court"

Belkin says two of those seats would "nullify" the fact that President Donald Trump's first nominee to the court, Justice Neil M. Gorsuch, won confirmation in 2017 only after Senate Republicans refused to advance President Barack Obama's nomination of Merrick B. Garland for the vacancy created by Justice Antonin Scalia's death in 2016.

Belkin and some other progressives believe that Trump's second nominee, Justice Brett M. Kavanaugh, should be effectively canceled out by adding a third and fourth new seat because the president lacks legitimacy or because of Republicans' hardball tactics to confirm Kavanaugh.

"The court is a partisan institution," Belkin says. "Nothing is going to change that."

Mark Tushnet, a professor at Harvard Law School who leads the advisory board of Pack the Courts, says that Democrats need to realize that if they are to achieve their policy goals on issues such as the environment, immigration and health care, the increasingly conservative-dominated federal courts, including the Supreme Court, likely stand in the way.

"You have to figure out some way to deal with a hostile Supreme Court," Tushnet says.

Other progressive groups that have been pushing to expand the court, among other radical ideas, include Demand Justice and Indivisible.

The groups' efforts began to show some traction in March. First, former US Attorney General Eric H. Holder Jr., who served under Obama, told an audience at Yale Law School that expansion of the court should be given serious consideration.

Soon after, Democratic presidential candidates began to offer thoughts on the idea.

Sens. Kirsten Gillibrand of New York, Kamala Harris of California and Elizabeth Warren of Massachusetts have said they would not rule out the idea, while former US Rep. Beto O'Rourke of Texas and Pete Buttigieg, the mayor of South Bend, Indiana, have embraced the concept of expanding the court to 15 members, with five nominated by a Republican president, five by a Democrat and five by unanimous consent of the other 10.

Buttigieg told a CNN town hall in March that he is trying to stop the Supreme Court from "sliding toward being viewed as a nakedly political institution. I'm for us contemplating whatever policy options will allow that to be possible."

Lessons from FDR's Plan

While legal experts say the idea of involving justices in choosing some of their peers would require a constitutional amendment, merely adding seats to the court could be done by passing a law.

The Judiciary Act of 1789 created a Supreme Court of one chief justice and five associate justices. An 1801 federal law reduced the size of the court to five justices, but the new administration of President Thomas Jefferson did not allow that law to go into effect.

The six-member court grew to seven in 1807, to nine in 1837 and to 10 in 1863. In 1866, Congress passed a law that would have reduced the court by attrition to seven members, though the size fell only to eight members by 1869, when Congress passed a law setting the size at nine, where it has remained since.

President Franklin Delano Roosevelt's famous "court-packing" plan came after he was re-elected in 1936, and after the Supreme Court had struck down many of his first-term New Deal programs. Roosevelt's proposal would have added a new justice for every sitting justice older than 70. (Six of the nine were then over 70, and thus the court might have grown to 15.)

Roosevelt's plan lacked support among many congressional Republicans and Democrats, and even Chief Justice Charles Evans Hughes worked against it behind the scenes. (At the time, the ABA held a referendum on court-packing that members overwhelmingly opposed.)

When the court shifted course in 1937 and began to uphold New Deal measures, any momentum for FDR's plan eroded further, and the president's plan died in Congress.

Belkin says historians have misconstrued the lessons of FDR's court-packing episode.

"I don't think what FDR did was a failure," he says. "Even though he didn't add justices, his plan did ultimately save the New Deal."

Jeff Shesol, a historian who wrote an authoritative book on FDR's court-packing plan, says "the sudden vogue for court-packing is that the appeal of the idea is very much the same as it had for Roosevelt. It feels like a quick fix."

"I understand the argument that Republicans have been smashing norms to such an extent that the court has been debased," adds Shesol, who was a speechwriter for President Bill Clinton and is the author of the 2010 book *Supreme Power: Franklin Roosevelt vs. The Supreme Court*. "But it seems to me to be destructive."

He says that if the Democrats win power in 2020 and increase the size of the court to 11 or 13 members, Republicans would likely vow to add even more justices when they returned to power to counter those additions.

"It's hard for me to see how the two parties don't then get into an arms race," Shesol says. Senate Majority Leader Mitch McConnell of Kentucky was critical of expanding the size of the court, saying on the Senate floor that "the far left has gone scrounging through the ash heap of American history, and they're bandying about that discredited fantasy from the 1930s."

In March, President Trump was asked whether he would consider an effort of his own to increase the size of the court. He said no. "The only reason [Democrats are] doing that is they want to try and catch up," Trump said at a Rose Garden news conference. "So if they can't catch up through the ballot box by winning an election, they want to try doing it in a different way. … It'll never happen."

Risking "Diffuse Support"

Neil S. Siegel, a Duke University law professor, says the Republicans' use of hardball tactics in recent confirmation battles is a factor that wasn't a factor with FDR's court-packing plan. But that doesn't justify the proposals of today, he says.

"Packing the court would substantially increase the public perception that the court is partisan and political in just the way, and to the same extent, that Congress is, and so would risk jettisoning the significant amount of diffuse support that the court retains," says Siegel, who served as a special counsel to Sen. Christopher A. Coons, a Delaware Democrat and Judiciary Committee member, for the confirmation hearings for Gorsuch and Kavanaugh.

He says the "legitimate" way to pack the court is to do what FDR ultimately had to settle for—winning elections and nominating and confirming justices of the president's choosing as vacancies arose.

"Indeed, had most liberals been as focused on the court in 2016 as some of them appear to be today, perhaps it is certain conservatives inside and outside Congress who would be talking about court-packing now," Siegel says.

Tushnet, who has debated the issue with Siegel, says he doesn't worry that proposals by progressives and Democrats to add to the court will motivate Republicans to retaliate because conservatives are already mobilized around the court.

As to whether any court-packing plan could really happen, Tushnet says, "I think talking about it is a way of expanding the conversation about the role of the Supreme Court as an obstacle to the substantive policies that Democrats want. That in itself is valuable."

14

Court-Packing Is Generally a Bad Idea

Ilya Somin

Ilya Somin is a professor of law at George Mason University, a researcher with the Cato Institute, and former co-editor of the Supreme Court Economic Review. His research focuses on constitutional and property law.

The concept of court-packing is a partisan political strategy using judicial appointments to protect certain laws or policies from hostile judicial review. If the party or faction in power rushes to seat as many friendly judges as possible on any open bench, their actions will be better protected from interference. However, such a strategy almost inevitably points toward a kind of partisan war of attrition around court appointments, thereby further politicizing and weakening the judiciary branch. The viewpoint suggests that we should worry more about this weakening of the judiciary than we should about the frustrating problems that arise with judicial review of law and policy.

The retirement of Justice Anthony Kennedy has stimulated renewed liberal interest in "court packing"—the idea of increasing the number of Supreme Court justices in order to get a majority more favorable to their views. Many on the left fear that this is the only way they can prevent a conservative majority from dominating the Court for a long time to come. While I can understand their distaste for conservative jurisprudence (and even

"The Case Against Court-Packing Revisited," by Ilya Somin, Reason Foundation, July 3, 2018. Reprinted by permission.

agree with it on some points), court-packing is a cure far worse than any likely disease.

Last year, ironically, it was a conservative court-packing plan that made waves in legal circles—one offered by famed conservative legal scholar Steven Calabresi (in a paper coauthored with Shams Hirji), who hoped to pack the lower federal courts with Republican judges. Most of what I wrote in criticism of the Calabresi-Hirji plan applies equally to today's progressive versions of the idea:

> *If either the Republicans... or the Democrats.... succeed in packing the courts, the opposing party is sure to do exactly the same thing the next time they control the White House and both Houses of Congress. This is even more likely if court-packing can be enacted through the reconciliation process (as Calabresi and Hirji argue), and thus requires only a narrow Senate majority to pass.*
>
> *Ending the norm against court-packing ensures that the judiciary will not serve as an effective check on the other branches of government at the very time when it is most likely to be needed: when one party holds both Congress and the presidency, and can thereby push through its agenda with relatively little opposition. Especially in a highly polarized era like our own, it is precisely at such times that the ruling party is [particularly] likely to violate constitutional constraints on its power in order to score victories against the hated opposition....*
>
> *[T]he case against court-packing does not depend on the proclivities of any one president. As James Madison famously warned us: "Enlightened statesmen will not always be at the helm." Indeed, dangerously unenlightened politicians are all too common. The norm against court-packing is an important bulwark against their depredations—and those of the political majorities who put them in power.*

I fully recognize that many Democrats regard court-packing as justified retaliation for the GOP's "theft" of the Supreme Court seat that went to Neil Gorsuch as a result of the Republican-controlled Senate's refusal to hold hearings and vote on Barack Obama nominee Merrick Garland. Republicans, in turn, argue that their treatment of Garland was justified by past Democratic misdeeds in the judicial nomination process (including refusal to hold hearings for a number of prominent GOP circuit court nominees), and that the Democrats themselves had signaled they would refuse to consider a GOP nominee in circumstances similar to those surrounding the Garland appointment. The truth is that, for a long time, both parties have shamelessly violated a variety of norms surrounding judicial nominations almost any time it seemed like they might gain an advantage to doing so. And both are equally shameless in shifting back and forth on procedural issues whenever the political winds dictate. The latest example is the contrast between GOP Senate leader Mitch NcConnell's insistence, in 2016, that the then-open Supreme Court seat should not be filled until after the November election, and his current claims that the present vacancy must be filled quickly, and certainly before the GOP might potentially lose its Senate majority in this fall's election.

But whatever we might think about the history of these shenanigans, court-packing is qualitatively different from any of them. Holding up nominees (as the GOP did with Garland), filibustering them (as the Democrats did with several Bush nominees, and as many—including Barack Obama—tried to do with Justice Samuel Alito), or "slow walking" them through the nomination process (many examples from both parties), are all potentially problematic. But all still leave the judiciary intact as a serious check on the power of the other branches of government. Court-packing, by contrast, would not. Once the norm against it is broken, both parties will resort to it whenever they have simultaneous control over Congress and the presidency, thereby foreclosing any significant judicial review of their policies.

When it was proposed last year, the Calabresi-Hirji plan sank like a stone. Even many on the right rejected it. That reaction showed the continued vitality of the norm against court-packing. But conservatives are likely to rethink their position if they believe liberal Democrats will pack the courts the first time they get a chance. And they will almost certainly do so (and retaliate in kind) if the Democrats actually do resort to court-packing the next time they get the chance.

Some liberal Democrats might still conclude that it's better to blow up judicial review than to leave that power to be exercised by a Court with a conservative majority. This would be an understandable, but shortsighted reaction. For all their serious differences and very real flaws, mainstream liberal and mainstream conservative jurists still agree on many important questions, including protection of a wide range of freedom of speech, basic civil liberties, and ensuring a modicum of separation of powers, among others. History shows that these are the sorts of restraints on government power that the executive (sometimes backed by Congress) is likely to break during times of crisis, or when they have much-desired partisan agendas to pursue. Such actions are especially likely if the president is a populist demagogue with authoritarian impulses. And, as the current occupant of the White House demonstrates, the safeguards against such people getting power are not nearly as strong as we might have thought before 2016. As specialists in comparative politics emphasize, it is no accident that court-packing is a standard tool of authoritarian populists seeking to undermine liberal democracy, recently used in such countries as Hungary, Turkey, and Venezuela.

As a libertarian, I have a long list of reservations about both conventional liberal judges and conventional conservative ones. But even if the judiciary is staffed by flawed jurists, it is still a valuable safeguard against illiberalism and authoritarianism.

While court-packing does not violate the Constitution, the norm against it has held for almost 150 years now, surviving even Franklin D. Roosevelt's 1937 effort to pack the Court, at a time when FDR was extremely popular and Democrats had large majorities in Congress. His plan was killed, in part, by congressional Democrats who feared the negative long-term consequences of acceding to it. As Democratic Senator Burton Wheeler put it in a speech attacking FDR's plan:

> *Create now a political court to echo the ideas of the Executive and you have created a weapon. A weapon which, in the hands of another President in times of war or other hysteria, could well be an instrument of destruction. A weapon that can cut down those guaranties of liberty written into your great document by the blood of your forefathers and that can extinguish your right of liberty, of speech, of thought, of action, and of religion. A weapon whose use is only dictated by the conscience of the wielder.*

That warning seems no less appropriate today than in the 1930s. Certainly, the current president and many of his likely successors don't strike me as the sorts of people in whose "conscience" we should put much faith.

It is also important to recognize that much of what liberals fear at the hands of a conservative Supreme Court majority is the undermining of judicial protection for rights of special importance to progressives, such as the right to abortion (imperiled by a possible overruling of *Roe v. Wade*) and the right to same-sex marriage (which would be undermined by an overruling of *Obergefell v. Hodges*). For reasons well summarized by Josh Barro, I think it's actually highly unlikely that *Obergefell* would be overruled. *Roe v. Wade* is, I believe, far more likely to be overturned, or at least seriously weakened.

But both these rights—and others valued by liberals—would be far more imperiled if the entire institution of judicial review is gutted by court-packing. That would ensure that these rights would never again get significant judicial protection—at least not if their adversaries control Congress and the White House. The same applies to a wide range of other constitutional rights, especially those that protect unpopular minorities, who are especially likely to face a hostile president and Congress, sooner or later. Like most liberals, I hated the Supreme Court's recent travel ban decision. But undermining judicial review through court-packing is a great way to ensure that future presidents will continue to be able to institute whatever discriminatory travel ban policies they want. A flawed Supreme Court decision can be overruled in the future, as many have been. It will be much harder to restore the institution of judicial review, once that is lost.

Court-packing might still be attractive to people who believe that it's more important to eliminate "bad" judicial review as an obstacle to beneficial policies, than to preserve the "good" kind as an obstacle to oppressive ones. That theory has advocates on both right and left. This longstanding issue cannot be fully settled in a blog post. But I believe the history of American government—and government elsewhere—shows we have more to fear from state oppression than from excessive exercise of judicial review. Given widespread voter ignorance and prejudice, majority public opinion—and the politicians it elects—often cannot be trusted to avoid deeply oppressive and unjust policies. Judicial review cannot prevent all such wrongs, but it has historically done a good deal to at least alleviate them.

Court-packing was a terrible idea when FDR advocated it in 1937 and when some conservatives pushed it last year. It remains a terrible idea today.

15

Liberals Have a Case for Expanding the Supreme Court

Miles Mogulescu

Miles Mogulescu is a producer, entertainment executive, political activist, and writer. He was formerly senior vice president at MGM.

In this polemic, the author gives voice to simmering liberal anger over Senate Majority Leader Mitch McConnell's aggressive tactics in filling federal court vacancies over the last several years, particularly during the Trump administration. The author argues that McConnell and Republicans' recalcitrant partisanship has gone far enough to justify extreme countermeasures. His primary suggestion is a direct expansion of the Supreme Court by the new administration to counter the influence of conservative justices who were appointed, in his judgment, to support the actions of an illiberal, undemocratic Republican Party.

Mitch McConnell has achieved his lifelong political dream: packing the Federal Courts, and especially the Supreme Court, with right-wing extremists, who thanks to him, now hold lifetime appointments.

The result: Even if the Democrats manage to win the Presidency, the House, and the Senate simultaneously, a Supreme Court with a young 5-4 right-wing majority could undermine voting rights,

"Expanding Supreme Court May Be Only Way to Protect Democracy," by Miles Mogulescu, OurFuture, March 14, 2019. https://ourfuture.org/20190314/expanding-size -of-supreme-court-may-be-only-way-to-protect-democracy. Licensed under CC BY 3.0.

environmental regulation, a woman's right to choose, and many other areas for decades to come.

McConnell subscribes to the premise that "the easiest way to change the law is to change the judges." As a result of refusal to consider Obama's appointment of Merrick Garland to the Supreme Court, his subsequent success in installing young right-wing ideologues like Neil Gorsuch and Brett Kavanaugh to the highest court in the land, as well as his packing Federal District and Appeals Courts with other right-wing ideologues, McConnell may have insured that his dead hand will continue to govern the nation's laws, long after he's gone from the Senate and even the planet.

Expand the Size of the Supreme Court

Faced with this prospect, some Democrats have raised the possibility of a fix that would formerly be verboten to speak about in polite Washington company—If Democrats win all three branches of government, they could, by a simple Congressional majority vote, increase the number of Supreme Court Justices from nine to eleven and change the Court's balance.

According to Daily Beast editor Sam Stein, no less a figure than former Attorney General Eric Holder told a group at Yale Law School that if Democrats win the Presidency and both Houses of Congress, they should consider adding additional seats to the Supreme Court. Holder's spokesman Patrick Rodenbush elaborated:

Attorney General Holder said that given the unfairness, unprecedented obstruction, and disregard of historical precedent by Mitch McConnell and Senate Republicans, when Democrats retake the majority they should consider expanding the Supreme Court to restore adherence to previously accepted norms for judicial nominations.

Brian Fallon, a former top aide to Holder, Charles Schumer, and Hillary Clinton, who heads a new organization called Demand Justice, stated,

We strongly believe that reforming the court—especially by expanding it—is the cornerstone for re-building American

democracy. The Kavanaugh court is a partisan operation, and democracy simply cannot function when stolen courts operate as political shills.

Democrats cannot sit back and accept the status quo of a partisan five-seat majority for the next 30 years. We don't consider those two seats that Trump has filled to be legitimate.

Ann Ravel, former Chair of the Federal Elections Commission, added,

I believe that the next Democratic administration should enlarge the Supreme Court, adding justices who will reverse the rigging of democracy. Today, the Court is controlled by justices chosen specifically because they'd listen to the rich and powerful. One of them sits in Justice Merrick Garland's rightful seat. Two others have been credibly accused of sexual misconduct. Why should these be the judges who sit on high and decide our rights and the meaning of our Constitution? To truly change our broken political process, we need a Court that believes that all of us should have a voice.

The prominence of the newly energized court expansion advocates may well force 2020 Democratic Presidential contenders to take a stand on the issue.

Congress Has a Constitutional Right to Add Justices

There will be predictable objections from Republicans and Washington elites (including some Democrats) that such a move is either unconstitutional, or is such a large break from traditional norms that it would be too divisive to be worth it.

The Constitutional argument may be quickly dismissed. Quite simply, there is nothing in the constitution that specifies the number of Supreme Court judges. Congress has the power to set the number. Congress has changed the number repeatedly: In 1801 Congress set the number of Justices at 5, increased it to 7 in 1807, 9 in 1837, and 10 in 1863, and in 1866 (to prevent Pres. Andrew Johnson, who was in the process of being impeached, from naming any new Justices) moved it back to 7. Then in 1869,

Congress set the number at 9, until, by refusing to even consider President Obama's nomination of the moderate Merrick Garland to replace the center-right Anthony Kennedy, Mitch McConnell and Senate Republicans decided that 8 Justices were sufficient for the time being.

So objections by McConnell and Republicans that changing the number of Justices would be an out of bounds effort to break norms and politicize the Court are hypocritical, or worse.

McConnell has already broken the norms beyond recognition. In concert with the right-wing Federalist Society and Heritage Foundation, McConnell has devoted the past 30 years to packing the Federal Courts with increasingly reactionary ideologues. Among the right-wing decisions decided by a bare 5-4 conservative majority are the 2000 decision to stop the Florida recount and install George W. Bush as President, the decision to gut key sections of the Voting Rights Act, the refusal to put limits on partisan gerrymandering, and *Citizens United*. By a single vote majority, the Supreme Court has spent the past several decades undermining American democracy.

"In this moment, only one side is honoring norms meaning there aren't really norms anymore," according to Pack the Courts Executive Director Aaron Belkin. Adding Justices could "restore democracy to our democracy," says Belkin.

FDR's Efforts

Some critics may refer back to FDR's failed 1936-37 attempt to add Justices in response to the Supreme Court overturning much of his New Deal legislation to combat the Great Depression. Roosevelt was accused of trying to "pack the court" and his plan was eventually defeated by a Democratic-controlled Congress.

But if FDR lost the battle to increase the Court's size, he won the war to change the Court's judicial philosophy to uphold the New Deal.

Three weeks after FDR first proposed increasing the Court size, Justice Owen Roberts switched sides to create a 5-4 generally pro-New Deal Supreme Court majority by upholding a minimum wage law that would previously have been found unconstitutional as infringing on the "right" to freely contract. Justice Robert's reversal was famously called "the switch in time that saved the nine." Ever since then, the Supreme Court has generally upheld the government's right to regulate the economy.

Even a failed attempt by a Democratic President could have an impact in moderating future Supreme Court decisions, as it did in the Roosevelt era.

Chief Justice Roberts is hardly a "moderate," as some assert, just because he provided the fifth vote to uphold the Affordable Care Act (while crippling it in key ways). He's been solidly in the right wing camp on most issues, including *Citizens United*, voting rights, and gun-owner rights, among other controversial issues.

But Roberts does seem to be an institutionalist, with concerns about maintaining the Supreme Court's legitimacy. Gorsuch and Kavanaugh are more aggressive conservative judicial activists than Roberts and may be more likely to see the Courts as a means of imposing their right-wing agenda, even against popular majorities.

It's possible that—faced with a credible threat to change the Court size—Roberts would avoid providing the 5th right-wing vote on highly divisive issues like overturning *Roe v. Wade*, or finding environmental regulations enacted by Federal agencies unconstitutional. It might not quite be "a switch in time to save the nine" but it could put a crimp on the most reactionary potential Supreme Court decisions.

Protect Democracy

By holding that corporations are persons, unlimited contributions to PACS are protected by the First Amendment, encouraging voter suppression by overturning key sections of the Voting Rights Act, and failing to limit partisan gerrymandering, the one vote conservative Court majority Court has undermined democracy and put its thumb on the scale to help Republicans get elected.

Given the relative youth of the conservative Justices, the Supreme Court could undermine democracy, overturn the will of Congress and regulatory agencies to combat climate change, and infringe a woman's right to choose for generations after Trump, McConnell, and many Republican Senators are dead and gone.

Threatening to, or actually, increasing the size of the court may be the only way to protect democracy. 2020 Democratic candidates may not be able to avoid this issue for long.

16

Court-Packing Threatens to Destroy the Entire Institution of Judicial Review

Ilya Somin

Ilya Somin is a professor of law at George Mason University, a researcher with the Cato Institute, and former co-editor of the Supreme Court Economic Review. His research focuses on constitutional and property law.

Most Americans understand that court-packing is an unusually aggressive, and dangerously inflammatory, political tactic. But despite the dangers, some liberals have become convinced that such aggressive tactics are necessary, given the level of abject intransigence that the Republican Party has demonstrated under the leadership of Senate Majority Leader Mitch McConnell. This viewpoint rejects that position and argues that the fallout from escalating political warfare will likely undermine anything liberals are able to gain from court-packing tactics.

In recent weeks, there has been growing support for court-packing on the left. A number of prominent liberal Democrats, including several presidential candidates, have either endorsed the idea of expanding the size of the Supreme Court to reverse the current 5-4 conservative majority among the justices, or at least indicated they are open to it. Those expressing such views include presidential candidates Pete Buttigieg, Kamala Harris, Elizabeth Warren and Kirsten Gillibrand. Former Obama administration

"Dangers of Growing Support for Court-Packing," by Ilya Somin, Reason Foundation, March 20, 2019. Reprinted by permission.

attorney General Eric Holder also argues that the idea should be "seriously" considered. Presidential candidate Beto O'Rourke has suggested a plan to increase the size of the court to fifteen justices: five Democrats, five Republicans, and five more justices selected by the other ten.

Liberal advocates of court-packing argue that it is a justifiable response to previous Republican bad behavior on judicial confirmations, most notably the GOP-controlled Senate's refusal to hold hearings on President Obama's nomination of Judge Merrick Garland in 2016, which eventually enabled to President Trump to fill the open seat with Justice Neil Gorsuch in 2017.

Both parties have engaged in skullduggery on judicial nominations in recent years, the GOP most certainly included. In my view, the refusal to consider Garland was understandable in light of previous Democratic actions (including their own refusal to hold hearings on a number of prominent Bush-era judicial nominees). But it is also true that it was a risky escalation of the judicial nomination wars.

Be that as it may, court-packing would be a dangerous step beyond previous judicial nomination shenanigans because, unlike them, it threatens to destroy the entire institution of judicial review, by creating a pattern of escalation under which each party would pack the court any time it simultaneously controls both Congress and the presidency. That would ensure that the Court would almost never rule against any significant initiative of the party in power, no matter how dangerous and unconstitutional. Prominent liberal Harvard Law School Professor Laurence Tribe summarizes the danger well:

> *Larry Tribe likewise argues against court-packing. "I'm not in favor of trying what FDR sought to do—and was rebuffed by the Democratic Senate for attempting," he tells me. "Obviously partisan Court-expansion to negate the votes of justices whose views a party detests and whose legitimacy the party doubts could trigger a tit-for-tat spiral that would endanger the Supreme Court's vital role in stabilizing the national political and legal system."*

Similarly, Democratic Senator and presidential candidate Cory Booker "caution[s] people about doing things that become a tit for tat throughout history… So when the Democrats expand it to 11, 12 judges, when Republicans have it, they expand it to 15 judges." Booker and Tribe are right. And indeed these sorts of structural concerns are exactly what led a Democratic-controlled Congress to bury Franklin D. Roosevelt's 1937 court-packing plan—the last serious attempt to expand the size of the Court in order to shift its ideology. Critics rightly feared that court-packing would create a Supreme Court subservient to whatever party controlled the presidency and Congress at the time.

As Democratic Senator Burton Wheeler put it in a speech on FDR's plan:

> *Create now a political court to echo the ideas of the Executive and you have created a weapon. A weapon which, in the hands of another President in times of war or other hysteria, could well be an instrument of destruction. A weapon that can cut down those guaranties of liberty written into your great document by the blood of your forefathers and that can extinguish your right of liberty, of speech, of thought, of action, and of religion. A weapon whose use is only dictated by the conscience of the wielder.*

For what it is worth, my opposition to court-packing is is not limited to plans put forward by liberal Democrats. I first wrote about the subject when prominent conservative law professor Steven Calabresi and his coauthor Shams Hirji put forward a plan for Republicans to pack the lower federal courts back in 2017. It was a bad idea when raised by some on the right two years ago, and it's no better now when it is gathering steam on the left.

Undermining judicial independence might be a feature of court-packing rather than a bug if you believe that judicial review does more harm than good, in any event (as do a few legal scholars on both the right and the left). Such people contend we would have a a freer and more just society if the courts let the political branches of government do as they please. I believe that is a dangerous delusion, for reasons I summarized here:

For all their serious differences and very real flaws, mainstream liberal and mainstream conservative jurists still agree on many important questions, including protection of a wide range of freedom speech, basic civil liberties, and ensuring a modicum of separation of powers, among others. History shows that these are the sorts of restraints on government power that the executive (sometimes backed by Congress) is likely to break during times of crisis, or when they have much-desired partisan agendas to pursue. Such actions are especially likely if the president is a populist demagogue with authoritarian impulses. And, as the current occupant of the White House demonstrates, the safeguards against such people getting power are not nearly as strong as we might have thought before 2016. As specialists in comparative politics emphasize, it is no accident that court-packing is a standard tool of authoritarian populists seeking to undermine liberal democracy, recently used in such countries as Hungary, Turkey, and Venezuela.

As a libertarian, I have a long list of reservations about both conventional liberal judges and conventional conservative ones. But even if the judiciary is staffed by flawed jurists, it is still a valuable safeguard against illiberalism and authoritarianism.

Some liberals who value judicial review generally might believe that conservative judges will not act to curb the abuses of Trump and other Republican presidents. If so, it might be better to risk blowing up the judiciary than allow conservatives to continue to have a majority on the Supreme Court.

It is indeed true that conservative judges have sometimes let Trump get away with violations of the Constitution, most notably in the egregious travel ban case. But conservative Republican judicial appointees (along with liberal Democratic ones) have done much to curb the administration's excesses in other important cases. Notable examples include the numerous rulings against Trump's attempts to coerce sanctuary cities, the recent Ninth Circuit decision against the administration's efforts to severely restrict migrants' opportunities to apply for asylum (authored by prominent conservative judge Jay Bybee), and a variety of decisions on such important issues as DACA, the administration's family-separation policy (struck down by a Republican-appointed judge who ordered the administration to reunite the separated children with their families), and freedom of speech. If Trump had had a free hand to pack the courts as he likes, things would likely have been much worse. And the same goes for future presidents inclined to abuse their power.

Some on the left argue that the Democrats can expand the size of the Court without generating retaliation in kind by Republicans if they repackage court-packing as "court balancing" or some other similar euphemism. This is unlikely to work. Those attracted to such ideas should consider whether they themselves would forego retaliation if the GOP tried to pull a similar trick.

Fortunately, the left is far from monolithic when it comes to court-packing. As the above quotes by Laurence Tribe and Cory Booker reveal, some liberals do recognize the danger. Other notable liberal critics of court-packing include former Obama White House Counsel Bob Bauer, columnist Damon Linker (who calls it "the dumbest Democratic idea yet") and well-known legal scholar Richard Primus. Whether Democrats actually move forward with court-packing the next time they have a chance to do so depends in large part on who becomes the next Democratic president and whether he or she decides to make this an important part of the party's agenda.

Some Democrats are instead promoting other, far more defensible, reforms to the Supreme Court. For example, Cory Booker has called for imposing 18-year term limits on the justices. I have no problem with that idea, which enjoys widespread (though certainly not universal) support from legal scholars on different sides of the political spectrum, such as Sanford Levinson on the left, and Steve Calabresi on the right. It would limit the power of individual justices without giving the president and Congress a blank check to pack the Court as they like.

Beto O'Rourke's plan to increase the size of the court to 15 justices (mentioned above) is far less problematic than standard court-packing proposals. Because it would require a balance between five Democratic and five Republican justices, with five more chosen by the first ten, it would not enable either the president or Congress to simply pack the Court with their own minions. There are, however, many practical problems with the plan. For example, it is not clear how the Democratic and Republican justices would be selected. In addition, if independents or third parties ever gain a significant foothold in Congress, they would be shut out of the judicial selection process. O'Rourke's proposal would also require a constitutional amendment to enact, which I think is highly unlikely to happen.

On the other side of the political spectrum, GOP Senator Marco Rubio plans to propose a constitutional amendment limiting the Supreme Court's membership to nine justices, which would prevent future court-packing. I am happy to support any such amendment. But I doubt that it can get enacted without some sort of quid pro quo for the Democrats. If it were up to me, I would be willing to pay a price to remove the danger of court-packing forever. But most Republican politician probably think otherwise.

For the moment, therefore, the main barrier to court-packing is the longstanding political norm against it. It has lasted for almost 150 years, and survived an assault by Franklin D. Roosevelt, one of the most popular presidents in American history. The next Democratic president is unlikely to be as commanding a figure as FDR was. On the other hand, the Democratic Party is arguably more ideologically cohesive now than in the 1930s, and the relative youth of the conservative Supreme Court justices (combined with increased life expectancy) makes it less likely that the Democrats can quickly retake control of the Supreme Court by "natural" means in the near future, than was the case back in 1937. And we should not underestimate the risk that liberal anger over the Court could help generate a "crisis of legitimacy" at some point in the next few years, which in turn could pave the way for court-packing. Nonetheless, I am guardedly optimistic that court-packing can still be staved off. But that happy outcome is more likely the more people understand the gravity of the danger.

17

How to Fix a Broken Nomination Process

E. Donald Elliott

E. Donald Elliott is adjunct professor of law at Yale University and a leading academic scholar in the fields of administrative and environmental law.

Depending on timing and the fact that justices are being appointed at younger ages and therefore have more time on the court, some US presidents have had an outsized influence over the makeup of the Supreme Court. One-term presidents Jimmy Carter and Donald Trump offer stark contrasts: Carter did not appoint any justices, while Trump successfully appointed three. Dwight Eisenhower appointed five during his two terms. This viewpoint suggests changing the law to grant each president two nominees per four-year term, which would see the number of justices fluctuating from 7 to 14.

President Donald Trump has nominated two Supreme Court justices during only 19 months in office.

Senate Majority Leader Mitch McConnell stated after Brett Kavanaugh's confirmation that Trump might have the opportunity to make a third nomination during one term in office. By the end of a possible second Trump term, he could choose a majority of the Supreme Court.

While the Supreme Court is not a representative body, justices on that court have strong, well-developed and significantly

"Fixing a Broken Process for Nominating US Supreme Court Justices," by E. Donald Elliott, The Conversation, October 15, 2018. https://theconversation.com/fixing-a-broken-process -for-nominating-us-supreme-court-justices-104629. Licensed under CC BY-ND 4.0.

different judicial philosophies and approaches to constitutional and statutory interpretation. Presidents openly admit that they make their nominations significantly based on these factors. Under the present system for nominating Supreme Court justices, voters in some elections have two or three times more influence over Supreme Court appointments than those in others.

This is anomalous and unfair because voters in one election usually have the same opportunity to elect government officers as those in another. But because a congressional statute fixes the size of the court at nine, some presidents will have the opportunity to nominate more Supreme Court justices than others, based on the happenstance of deaths or resignations. We think this is backwards: Each president should get an equal number of appointments per elected term and the size of the court should fluctuate over time as vacancies occur.

Fixing this phenomenon does not require a constitutional amendment. We are legal scholars who have written across a broad swath of areas including constitutional law. We believe Congress could pass a law providing that a president gets two Supreme Court appointments per four-year term in office.

The Constitution does not dictate the size of the Supreme Court; Congress does.

This new system would mean that the number of nominations a president gets would no longer fluctuate depending upon the vagaries of deaths and vacancies on the bench.

Unequal Terms

Even after states ratified the 22nd Amendment to limit US presidents to two terms in 1951, some presidents have had more influence on the court than others.

From 1952 through 1992, we calculated that on average presidents nominated two Supreme Court justices per four-year term who were successfully confirmed. From 1992 to 2016, that dropped to only one per term.

The court typically includes justices nominated by four or five different presidents, and confirmed by six or seven different Senates so that it reflects the political values of the country over a long period of time. In addition, most of the time, the court makes decisions based on constitutional, statutory and regulatory texts, historical sources and precedents reflecting an accumulated wisdom of the law over an even longer period of time.

The current system is no longer working as intended, perhaps because justices are being appointed at a younger age yet life expectancy is increasing. Consequently, some presidents can exercise vastly disproportionate influence over Supreme Court appointments for decades after their terms of office have expired.

The timing of when presidents get to nominate Supreme Court justices depends on when a justice dies or decides to retire. A congressional statute currently fixes the number of justices at nine. Congress could change that because under the Constitution, Congress regulates the size of the court.

From 1791 until 1807, the Supreme Court consisted of only six justices. A seventh was added in 1807, an eighth and ninth were added in 1837, and a 10th in 1866.

Then in 1869, Congress passed a statute reducing the number back to the current nine. At that time, a 50-year-old male nominated to the Supreme Court had a life expectancy of only 71 years. Today, justices often serve well into their 80s and life expectancy for a 50-year-old male is now 80, and for a 50-year-old female is 83.

A New Way

Under our proposal, Congress could pass a law that stipulates a president would get two nominees, and only two nominees, to the Supreme Court per four-year term. If that nominee were rejected by the Senate, the president would get to keep nominating until one was successfully confirmed. A death or resignation from the court would not entitle a president to name additional justices.

Some might ask, what happens when the Senate refuses to consider a nomination as it did with President Barack Obama's nomination of Judge Merrick Garland to the Supreme Court?

Under our proposal, the Senate would have a legally binding obligation to confirm two nominees each presidential term.

Of course, the Senate could still thumb their noses at any presidential nominee, as it did with Garland.

We doubt that this would happen. First, under our proposal, the president does not have to wait for a death or retirement of a justice to nominate. Instead, the president controls the time frame. If presidents make the nominations within several months of their election, we doubt that many Senates would have the temerity to vote down nominees for four years. The argument for delaying confirmation that has emerged since the unsuccessful Garland nomination has been the Senate controlled by the opposition party does not confirm nominees to the Supreme Court within a year of an upcoming presidential election. As presidents would have the right to make nominations as soon as they assumed office, the Merrick Garland problem will likely never happen again.

But suppose the Senate simply refused to consider a president's nominee either within one year of the presidential election or even before that—what then?

We suggest that Congress pass a statute requiring the Senate Judiciary Committee to hold hearings on any presidential nominee within two months. They would also be required to bring the issue to the floor for a roll call vote within a reasonable time, say four to six months of the nomination.

Failure to meet these deadlines would result in automatic confirmation. Any senator could enforce these requirements.

Some might think that this approach infringes on the constitutional powers of the Senate to make its own rules. We think it would be constitutional, as it gives the Senate a fair opportunity to "advise and consent" as required by the Constitution.

Alternatively, if the Senate fails to meet these deadlines, the statute could imitate the procedures mandated by the Budget

Reconciliation Act and require the Senate to bring the nominee to the floor for a vote within a set period of time and prohibit filibuster, as the Senate has now done for judicial nominees.

A Bigger Supreme Court

If such a statute had been in effect starting in 1952, the size of the Supreme Court would have fluctuated between seven and 14 justices. Each presidential election would have had equal weight in determining the composition of the court.

This system might reduce the incentive for justices to delay resigning so that certain presidents do not get a nominee, or for the Senate to stonewall a nominee until the next president takes office. Controversy surrounding some individual appointments could diminish.

Other scholars have criticized the current size of the court as too small because it leads to too many 5-4 decisions. These undermine the democratic legitimacy of the court, they argue, by suggesting that rather than applying law objectively, a single swing justice is deciding controversial issues for the country.

Many other notable courts are larger than ours. The Supreme Court of the United Kingdom, created in 2005, has 12 members. The European Union's highest court has 28 members.

This is not to say that we view the Supreme Court as a representative or legislative body. We believe judges should be constrained by texts. But within those constraints, justices do exercise judgment.

No good reason exists why some presidential elections should count for two or three times as much as others in determining how we are governed.

Organizations to Contact

The editors have compiled the following list of organizations concerned with the issues debated in this book. The descriptions are derived from materials provided by the organizations. All have publications or information available for interested readers. The list was compiled on the date of publication of the present volume; the information provided here may change. Be aware that many organizations take several weeks or longer to respond to inquiries, so allow as much time as possible.

American Bar Association (ABA)
1050 Connecticut Avenue NW
Suite 400
Washington, DC 20036
(202) 662-1000
email: service@americanbar.org
website: www.americanbar.org

The American Bar Association is dedicated to preserving and enhancing the legal profession in America by advocating for quality legal education and promoting professional competence. The ABA also works to increase public understanding of and respect for the rule of law, the legal process, and the role of the legal profession.

American Center for Law and Justice (ACLJ)
PO Box 90555
Washington, DC 20090-0555
(800) 342-2255
email: https://aclj.org/contact-us
website: www.aclj.org

American Center for Law and Justice is a tax-exempt, not-for-profit, religious corporation as defined under Section 501(c)(3) of the Internal Revenue Code, specifically dedicated to the ideal that religious freedom and freedom of speech are inalienable, God-given rights. The center's purpose is to engage legal, legislative, and cultural issues by implementing an effective strategy of advocacy, education, and litigation to ensure that those rights are protected under the law. The organization has participated in numerous cases before the Supreme Court, Federal Court of Appeals, federal district courts, and various state courts regarding freedom of religion and freedom of speech.

The American Civil Liberties Union (ACLU)

125 Broad Street, 18th Floor
New York NY 10004
(212) 549-2500
website: www.aclu.org

For nearly 100 years, the ACLU has been the nation's guardian of liberty, working in courts, legislatures, and communities to defend and preserve the individual rights and liberties that the Constitution and the laws of the United States guarantee all Americans.

Bill of Rights Institute

1310 North Courthouse Road #620
Arlington, VA 22201
(703) 894-1776
email: info@billofrightsinstitute.org
website: http://www.billofrightsinstitute.org/

Established in September 1999, the Bill of Rights Institute is a nonprofit educational organization that works to engage, educate, and empower individuals with a passion for the freedom and opportunity that exist in a free society. The institute develops educational resources and programs for a network of more than 50,000 educators and 70,000 students nationwide.

Church State Council
2686 Townsgate Road
Westlake Village, CA 91361
(805) 413-7396
website: www.churchstate.org

The Church State Council provides legal and counseling services to those suffering religious discrimination or harassment and files briefs in appellate courts involving important religious freedom issues. The council monitors legislation in its five-state southwestern territory and mobilizes effective grassroots responses to both state and federal legislation impacting religious freedom.

Constitutional Rights Foundation (CRF)
601 S. Kingsley Drive
Los Angeles, CA 90005
(213) 487-5590
email: crf@crf-usa.org
website: www.crf-usa.org

CRF is a nonprofit, nonpartisan, community-based organization dedicated to educating America's young people about the importance of civic participation in a democratic society. Under the guidance of a board of directors chosen from the worlds of law, business, government, education, the media, and the community, CRF develops, produces, and distributes programs and materials to teachers, students, and public-minded citizens all across the nation.

The Federalist Society
1776 I Street NW
Suite 300
Washington, DC 20006
(202) 822-8138
email: info@fedsoc.org
website: www.fedsoc.org

The Federalist Society for Law and Public Policy Studies is a group of conservatives and libertarians dedicated to reforming the current legal order. Members are committed to the principles that the state exists to preserve freedom, that the separation of governmental powers is central to the US Constitution, and that the province of the judiciary is to determine what the law is, rather than what it should or could be.

First Amendment Center
Freedom Forum Institute
300 New Jersey Avenue NW
Suite 800
Washington, DC 20001
(202) 292-6290
email: firstamendmentcenter@newseum.org
website: www.firstamendmentcenter.org

The First Amendment Center supports the First Amendment and builds understanding of its core freedoms through education, information, and entertainment. The center serves as a forum for the study and exploration of free-expression issues, including freedom of speech, of the press, and of religion, and the rights to assemble and to petition the government. Founded by John Seigenthaler, the First Amendment Center is an operating program of the Freedom Forum and is associated with the Newseum and the Diversity Institute.

National Constitution Center
Independence Mall
525 Arch Street
Philadelphia, PA 19106
(215) 409-6600
email: education@constitutioncenter.org
website: www.constitutioncenter.org

The National Constitution Center is the first and only institution in America established by Congress to "disseminate information about the United States Constitution on a nonpartisan basis in order to increase the awareness and understanding of the Constitution among the American people." The Constitution Center brings the United States Constitution to life by hosting interactive exhibits and constitutional conversations and inspires active citizenship by celebrating the American constitutional tradition.

United States Courts

Administrative Office of the United States Courts
One Columbus Circle NE
Washington, DC 20544
(202) 502-2600
email: https://www.uscourts.gov/contact-us
website: www.uscourts.gov

The United States Federal Courts were established under Article III of the Constitution to administer justice within the jurisdiction established by the Constitution and Congress. Federal courts hear cases involving the constitutionality of a law, cases involving a dispute between states, and bankruptcy cases.

The United States Supreme Court

1 First Street NE
Washington, DC 20543
(202) 479-3000
email: www.supremecourt.gov/contact/contact_pio.aspx
website: www.supremecourt.gov

The United States Supreme Court is the highest venue in the nation for legal cases, appeals, and controversies. As final arbiter of the law, the court is responsible for protecting the American promise of justice under the law. The court consists of a chief justice and eight associate justices, who are nominated by the president of the United States with the consent of the Senate.

Bibliography

Books

Lawrence Baum. *Ideology in the Supreme Court.* Princeton, NJ: Princeton University Press, 2017.

Joan Biskupic. *The Chief: The Life and Turbulent Times of Chief Justice John Roberts.* New York, NY: Basic Books, 2019.

Michael Bobelian. *Battle for the Marble Palace: Abe Fortas, Earl Warren, Lyndon Johnson, Richard Nixon and the Forging of the Modern Supreme Court.* Tucson, AZ: Schaffner Press, Inc., 2019.

Erwin Chemerinsky. *The Case Against the Supreme Court.* New York, NY: Penguin Books, 2015.

Adam Cohen. *Supreme Inequality: The Supreme Court's Fifty-Year Battle for a More Unjust America.* New York, NY: Penguin Press, 2020.

Michael J. Graetz and Linda Greenhouse. *The Burger Court and the Rise of the Judicial Right.* New York, NY: Simon and Schuster, 2016.

Jan Crawford Greenburg. *Supreme Conflict: The Inside Story of the Struggle for Control of the United States Supreme Court.* New York, NY: Penguin Press, 2007.

Mollie Hemingway and Carrie Severino. *Justice on Trial: The Kavanaugh Confirmation and the Future of the Supreme Court.* Washington, DC: Regnery Publishing, 2019.

David A. Kaplan. *The Most Dangerous Branch: Inside the Supreme Court in the Age of Trump.* New York, NY: Broadway Books, 2018.

Mark C. Miller. *Judicial Politics in the United States.* New York, NY: Routledge, 2015.

Ian Millhiser. *Injustices: The Supreme Court's History of Comforting the Comfortable and Afflicting the Afflicted.* New York, NY: Bold Type Books, 2016.

Damon Root. *Overruled: The Long War for Control of the US Supreme Court.* New York, NY: St. Martin's Press, 2014.

Ilya Shapiro. *Supreme Disorder: Judicial Nominations and the Politics of America's Highest Court.* New York, NY: Gateway Editions, 2020.

Geoffrey R. Stone and David A. Strauss. *Democracy and Equality: The Enduring Constitutional Vision of the Warren Court.* New York, NY: Oxford University Press, 2020.

Jeffrey Toobin. *The Nine: Inside the Secret World of the Supreme Court.* New York, NY: Anchor Books, 2008.

Mary Ziegler. *Abortion and the Law in America: Roe v. Wade to the Present.* New York, NY: Cambridge University Press, 2020.

Periodicals and Internet Sources

Joan Biskupic, "Samuel Alito's Viral Speech Signals Where Conservative Supreme Court Is Headed," CNN, November 13, 2020. https://www.cnn.com/2020/11/13/politics/samuel -alito-supreme-court-federalist-society-speech-analysis /index.html

Scott S. Boddery and Charles A. Phillips, "A Solution to the Politicization of the Supreme Court," *The Hill*, November 6, 2020. https://thehill.com/blogs/congress-blog /judicial/524775-a-solution-to-the-politicization-of-the -supreme-court

Ronald Brownstein, "The Supreme Court Is Colliding with a Less-Religious America," *Atlantic*, December 3, 2020. https://www.theatlantic.com/politics/archive/2020/12/how -supreme-court-champions-religious-liberty/617284/

Andrew Chung, "US Supreme Court Not Politicized, Says Chief Justice Roberts," Reuters, September 24, 2019. https://www .reuters.com/article/us-usa-court-chiefjustice/u-s -supreme-court-not-politicized-says-chief-justice-roberts -idUSKBN1WA08F

Charlie Dent, "Democrats Also Play Politics with Supreme Court Seats," CNN, September 23, 2020. https://www.cnn .com/2020/09/23/opinions/scotus-democrats-republicans -hipocrisy-dent/index.html

Eric Hamilton, "Politicizing the Supreme Court," *Stanford Law Review*, August 2012. https://www.stanfordlawreview.org /online/politicizing-the-supreme-court/

Adam Liptak, "Supreme Court Starts Term with Case on the Politics of Judging," *New York Times*, October 5, 2020. https://www.nytimes.com/2020/10/05/us/politics/supreme -court-judges-ideology.html

Jemima McEvoy, "Parties Fight Over Politicization of Supreme Court, 'Losing the Trust of the American People,'" *Forbes*, October 12, 2020. https://www.forbes.com/sites /jemimamcevoy/2020/10/12/parties-fight-over -politicization-of-supreme-court-losing-the-trust-of-the -american-people/?sh=618ee0274451

Alex Pareene, "Supreme Court Justices Are Politicians, Too," *New Republic*, October 14, 2020. https://newrepublic.com /article/159744/amy-coney-barrett-conservative-judges -politicans

Ilya Shapiro, "Just Accept It: The Supreme Court Has Always Been Political," The Cato Institute, September 26, 2020. https://www.cato.org/publications/commentary/just-accept -it-supreme-court-has-always-been-political

Rachel Shelden, "The Supreme Court Used to Be Openly Political. It Traded Partisanship for Power," *Washington Post*, September 25, 2020. https://www.washingtonpost

.com/outlook/supreme-court-politics-history/2020/09/25
/b9fefcee-fe7f-11ea-9ceb-061d646d9c67_story.html

Mark Sherman, "Politics Has Way of Finding Supreme Court
Eager to Avoid It," AP News, October 8, 2020. https://
apnews.com/article/election-2020-virus-outbreak-donald
-trump-amy-coney-barrett-elections-5769268d6a1964f420e
696428ad2e5a9

Elizabeth Slattery, "The Way to Stop Politicizing the Supreme
Court," The Heritage Foundation, April 8, 2020. https://
www.heritage.org/courts/commentary/the-way-stop
-politicizing-the-supreme-court

John A. Tures, "Partisan Supreme Court Battles Are As Old As
the United States Itself," The Conversation, September 29,
2020. https://theconversation.com/partisan-supreme-court
-battles-are-as-old-as-the-united-states-itself-146657

James D. Zirin, "Beyond Court Packing: The Supreme Court
Has Always Been Political," *Time*, November 2, 2020.
https://time.com/5906442/court-packing-election-history/

Index